CREATING EVER-COOL

Creating

EVER-COOL
A Marketer's Guide to a Kid's Heart

Gene Del Vecchio

PELICAN PUBLISHING COMPANY
Gretna 1997

The word "Pelican" and the depiction of a pelican are trademarks
of Pelican Publishing Company, Inc., and are registered
in the U.S. Patent and Trademark Office.

Library of Congress Cataloging-in-Publication Data

Del Vecchio, Gene.
   Creating ever-cool: a marketer's guide to a kid's heart / Gene
Del Vecchio.
     p.   cm.
   ISBN 1-56554-256-8
   1. Child consumers. 2. Advertising and children 3. Children-
-Attitudes. I. Title. II. Title: Kid quest.
HF5415.32.D45   1997
658.8'34'083—DC21   97-1660
                                        CIP

Illustrations by Damian Fulton

Manufactured in the United States of America

Published by Pelican Publishing Company, Inc.
1101 Monroe Street, Gretna, Louisiana 70053

To my precious children, Matthew and Megan,
who have kept me young at heart; my wife, Linda,
who kindly tolerates the child within all of us;
and to my parents, who had the arduous task
of raising such a challenging kid.

Contents

Preface

Children's Television Workshop, the originator of "Sesame Street," has helped educate more than 120 million children worldwide. Eight percent of the American population visits McDonald's on an average day. Two Barbie dolls are sold every second somewhere in the world. By all measures, this is success!

People who helped create and develop brands such as these understand what most others do not. They understand the timeless, emotional needs that all children share. They know that children seek to gain control over a world they have yet to master. They understand children's innermost fantasies. Some also know the fears children seek to conquer. And they use such knowledge and more to create brands that touch children's hearts, thus satisfying the eternal needs held within. Importantly, they realize that their brands are not merely comprised of physical product features—an educational program, a burger and fries, a plastic doll. Instead, their brands are really about a relationship, and about a role that their brands play in a child's life.

Successful kid marketers also know how to keep their brands continuously fresh so that kids will look upon them as *cool* year after year. I call such brands "Ever-Cools," and while many marketers have tried to attain such status for their brands, only a few have succeeded because only a handful of marketers know how to do it well.

Creating Ever-Cool is about the timeless truths about children, about the emotional needs that demand satisfaction, and about the brands that have attempted to satisfy them year after year. It is your guide to the very heart of the child. Its intent is to open the eyes of those who attempt to market to children, thus allowing them to see a kids' world as kids see it, and to feel as kids feel.

Part I provides an overview of the magnitude of the kids' market, as well as the formula for achieving Ever-Cool. Part II probes the essence of the child's timeless psyche filled with needs and desires demanding satisfaction. Part III discusses a kid's world and culture, comprised of trends and fads that will help the marketer keep a brand eternally fresh while expanding its role within a child's life. Part IV reviews the tools marketers can use to develop the best possible kid brands and marketing programs. It also reviews issues related to ethics, for in a marketer's rush to fulfill a child's emotional needs and desires, care must be taken to ensure that the child is not harmed in the process.

The knowledge in *Creating Ever-Cool* comes from my many years of experience at Ogilvy & Mather, working in many kid categories such as toys, foods, candy, and entertainment. I have been involved with hundreds of studies with children. I have sat on the floor and looked them right in the eyes, watched them from behind one-way mirrors, heard what they said, and speculated about what they really meant. *Creating Ever-Cool* also draws upon the professional and personal insights of marketers all across the country, both inside and outside of Ogilvy & Mather, who have used their knowledge to create and develop brands.

This book will help you do the same. It will give you a better understanding of how you can fulfill a child's emotional needs and to continue to fulfill his needs year after year. When you fully understand how this process works, you will have succeeded in your battle to win a child's heart, and your brand will have attained Ever-Cool.

Acknowledgments

Many people have shaped the outcome of this book by providing me with raw information, insights, or a combination of both. Without them, this undertaking would never have been completed.

I would first like to thank the planning and research team at Ogilvy & Mather in Los Angeles. They uncovered the vast assortment of facts and figures used throughout this book. Headed by Janet Lin-Armstrong, the team also included Sandy Comstock, Tabitha Ji, and Irene Nomoto. Together, they conduct more than fifty studies a year with children, so their knowledge is vast.

I am forever in debt to a review committee I established to provide insights on early drafts of *Creating Ever-Cool*. It was comprised of kid-marketing experts across several of Ogilvy & Mather's kid businesses. The committee included Freddy Bee, Robert Hay, Brenda Hillhouse, Maya Levinson, Noah Manduke, and Rick Roth. Their thoughts were invaluable.

I would also like to thank other kid experts who, over my career, have added a tremendous number of insights to my own understanding of kids and kid marketing. Little by little, experience by experience, they helped me see a child's world. They are Alan Fine, Damian Fulton, Alice Germanetti, Elaine Haller, James Hayden, Barbara Lui,

Sujata Luther, Marty Miller, Scott Shaw, and Sandy Zachary. No one knows more about a kid's heart than they do. A very special thanks to Damian Fulton who also provided the wonderfully clever illustrations used throughout *Creating Ever-Cool*.

Roper Starch Worldwide, Simmons, and The Zandl Group kindly provided added information regarding the kids' market, for which I am also very grateful.

Special thanks must also go to Nina Kooij, Editor in Chief at Pelican; to Christine Descant, Assistant Editor at Pelican; and to my agent Laura Tucker of Richard Curtis Associates. Without their support, this book would still be but notes collecting about my ankles.

Finally, I am in debt to my boss, Jerry McGee, who at lunch a couple years ago turned to me and said, "Gene, just put all that stuff you know about kids in a book."

And so I have.

CREATING EVER-COOL

PART I
Introduction

Introduction

Unlike ages past when children were expected to be seen but not heard, today we live in the age of children. Their opinions are both voiced and appreciated. These opinions reflect a vast array of needs and desires whose impact ripples through our society and impacts family interaction, public policy, educational reform, the legal system, and commerce. Kids' influence in the marketplace is such that businesses that do not listen to children's opinions will not reach their full potential and many will assuredly fail. For while Mom and Dad remain the primary purchaser and gatekeeper for many goods and services brought into the home, they spend a lot of time listening to their children. They appreciate their thoughts, their input, and their preferences.

That is where our introduction begins. Chapter 1 provides an overview of kid influence: its immense size, the many industries it touches, as well as the manner in which it increases as children age. The chapter demonstrates that such influence is a powerful force to be both reckoned with and respected.

But such knowledge is not nearly enough, for while many marketers are at least partially aware of the power of kid influence in the marketplace, they have not been able to harness that influence for themselves. They do not know all of the child's innermost, emotional needs and desires that will help them create brands. And even if they are fortunate enough to create a successful brand, most marketers find it difficult to keep the brand contemporary and successful year after year. They do not apply what I call the Ever-Cool formula of success. That is the purpose of Chapter 2. It reveals the Ever-Cool formula as the beginning of true knowledge and as a beacon that will show marketers the path to creating long-term brands. It is the first critical step toward winning a kid's heart.

1

Kidquake:
A Turbulence Measuring
More Than $160 Billion

Yesteryear

I WAS BORN in the United States in 1955, near the height of the Baby Boom, which would eventually number some 76 million births. My youth, as well as those of my cohorts, bloomed in the sixties, and I took full advantage of it. There were fast, two-wheeler bikes; rollerskates and skateboards, each with the original metal—not urethane— wheels; long summer vacations; the ice-cream truck; comic books; Little League; and so much more.

During that time, a few innovative marketers, mostly in the toy and entertainment fields, began to focus upon and truly target the kid segment. Mattel was one, introducing the Barbie doll in 1959. Hasbro was another, introducing G.I. Joe in 1964. Disney was present with such creations as *Cinderella* (1950), *Lady and the Tramp* (1955), *Sleeping Beauty* (1959), and *Mary Poppins* (1964). Programming designed to attract kid viewers appeared as well, and included such shows as "Romper Room" and "Bozo the Clown," and later "The Brady Bunch" and "The Partridge Family."

But despite such early efforts, by today's standards, baby boomers were relatively ignored by most marketers. Many businesses were doing all they could just to meet the growing consumer demands of adults. Cars, suburban homes, and products to fill those homes were keeping manufacturers

**No, No, No! For the last time,
you may not have any rye bread.**

quite busy. This left few resources for most companies to address children directly.

Today

Yet in the past few decades, business has changed substantially. The demand for adult goods and services has proven not to be endless. Competition has grown. Marketers from many areas have realized that they needed to address a multitude of demographics in order to keep their businesses alive and growing. Concurrently, baby boomers such as myself came of age, struggling to make a place for themselves and their families in an adult world. So we, as every generation before us, have strived to make our children's lives richer and more fulfilling in every conceivable way. That meant more and varied experiences in education, social interaction, sports, culture, and just plain old excitement. We also had fewer children, which allowed dual-working boomer couples to spend more per child. And as some boomers divorced and remarried, it actually *added* to a child's list of gift-givers through an extended family network of step-parents, step-grandparents, and step-siblings. With almost four million children being born every year, the impact has been sizeable.

The Kidquake

These two trends, the marketers' need to find new audiences and the baby boomers' shifting demographics, have sparked a *kidquake* of kid-directed goods and services. And its force has rumbled throughout the marketing terrain. "Kids exert a tremendous amount of influence in everything from supermarket purchases and eating out to the hottest fashion trends and the best movies to see," says Rebecca McPheters, president and chief executive officer at Simmons, a leading market research company. Hilton Hotels, for example, has run summer promotions that provided toy boxes for use by children at some 80 Hilton "Vacation Station" hotels. Delta developed a kids' club called the Fantastic Flyers Program. ConAgra introduced Kid Cuisine, a line of kid-oriented frozen meals. "In conjunction with the fact that they have billions of dollars of their own to spend, the kids' market is a powerful revenue source," McPheters concludes.

Translated into precise dollars and cents, it is staggering. One specialist in kid marketing, so reported *Youth Markets ALERT*, estimated that the 34 million kids ages 4 to 12 receive an astonishing $15 billion a year. Of that, they spend about $11 billion in such categories as snacks, sweets, toys/games, and clothing and save about $4 billion. And beyond their own income, children also influence the purchase of more than $160 billion in *family* goods and services. And there is no abatement in sight as some estimate that kid wealth has been growing at a rate of 20 percent a year.

The influence children exert is stretched across a broad range of categories as shown in Table #1-1. It includes arenas where kid influence is expected such as in cereal (73 percent of children age 6 to 12 have "a lot or some" influence), dolls (71 percent), and frozen pizza (48 percent), to categories where such influence might be more surprising such as in shampoo (42 percent) and hotel selection (20 percent). Clearly, kids are a powerful lobby, voting with their own dollars and those of their parents, the results of which determine the brands that will live and the brands that will die.

As marketers continue to speak to children, and do so with appeals that inspire a child's interest, we might expect the percentages in Table #1-1 to actually rise. Case in point: McDonald's assuredly increased the amount of kid influence in the quick-service restaurant category with the introduction of the Happy Meal. This provided an incentive for a child to be of even more influence in the category than previously. In fact, the lowest "influence" percentages you see in Table #1-1 may represent the greatest opportunities for marketers, because they might be indicative of the arenas that have yet to fully and successfully speak to children.

Table #1-1

Degree of Influence

Influence: Kids Age 6-12

Product Category	A Lot	Some	A Lot/Some Total
Fast Food Restaurant	38%	36%	74%
Cold Cereals	43%	30%	73%
Movies	42%	30%	72%
Dolls	50%	21%	71%
Candy Bars/Packs	43%	25%	68%
Amusement Park	39%	29%	68%
Sneakers/Athletic Shoes	46%	19%	65%
Basketball (purchase of)	44%	19%	63%
Jeans	35%	24%	59%
Frozen Novelty Treats	26%	29%	55%
Toothpaste	25%	26%	51%
Regular Cola	26%	25%	51%
Potato Chips	21%	30%	51%
Shopping Stores	21%	28%	49%
Frozen Pizza	20%	28%	48%
Flavored Gelatin	17%	29%	46%
Shampoo	21%	21%	42%
Peanut Butter	15%	26%	41%
Vacation Destination	16%	23%	39%
Vacation Hotel	7%	13%	20%
Personal Computer/Home	7%	9%	16%

Source: 1995 Simmons Kid Study. Based on families of 6-12 year olds whose children use items listed. Scale included a lot, some, a little, and none.

The Ways of Influence

How do children influence purchases? It is easy. They simply ask their parents to buy certain items—and not to buy others. They ask, urge, and bargain. And they are good at it. Such requests have always been part of the kid/parent interaction and always will be. For as soon as a child is able to point with a finger, let alone talk, he begins to make his preferences known as he glides down the grocery aisle in the seat of a shopping cart.

In early years, when the child is about three or younger, requests are often random and not very specific. The child will ask for many things within his sight, then forget about the last request and concentrate on the next. This is evident, for example, every Christmas as the child requests the most recent toy seen on television. Then, a moment later, he will often forget about that toy and focus instead on the next one, which creates yet another request. The requests of this younger child are also often generic, for he is apt to ask for a toy car or a bike, rather than for a specific brand of toy car or bike.

When the child grows older, however, requests become more exact as he develops true preferences and is able to articulate them. Hence, an eight-year-old girl may want a Baywatch Barbie doll and none other. And while other enticements may make her rethink her request, she is now old enough to know that she will not get everything—so she is more likely to be more selective with the requests she makes. At that point in time, she is an increasingly savvy consumer with clear preferences and the wherewithall to know the limitations.

The Influence Curve

Exhibit #1-1 charts this relationship into a generalized influence curve. A child under the age of four does not have significant influence over purchase decisions for specific brands, which often results in the marketer speaking only to the parent. But a child's influence increases substantially in just a few years as speech and preferences form. In kid-dominated categories such as toys, kid influence can account for as much as 70 percent of a toy's purchase by the time the child is seven or eight, making child-directed marketing the primary focus. A secondary adult effort might still be warranted to communicate a benefit to parents (e.g., value), if the resources to reach them are available. If a brand's appeal falls within these extremes, say for children ages four to six, a marketer may decide to speak to both audiences depending on the nature of the product, the available budget, and the specific circumstances.

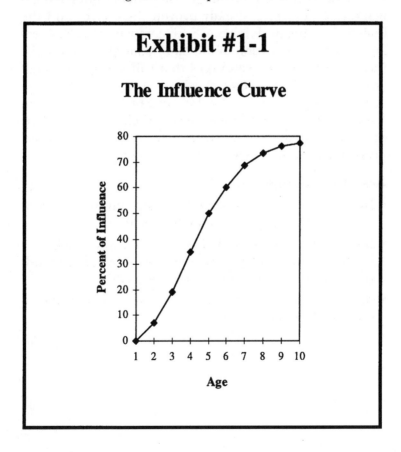

Exhibit #1-1

The Influence Curve

The Battle

The primary focus of this book is to increase the marketer's ability to develop brands and market them to those children old enough to consider them and to articulate their preferences—hence, children ages four and older. That is where the marketer's battle is most fierce, for in a world where children are both increasingly influential and increasingly selective, competition is keen.

Yet most marketers are still new to the kid arena. They look at the obstacles, the hurdles, the maze that reflects a kid's desires. They see the tough competition, those few kid marketers who have already proven themselves and the brands that already dominate. Such competition is frightening. At stake is a portion of the more than $160 billion pie. But it is not size or resources that will win it, for small brands can and do become massive overnight.

The battle will be won by the company that best understands kids, their emotional needs, their fantasies, their dreams, their desires. Such knowledge is the mightiest weapon in a marketer's arsenal to win a child's heart.

Brand Challenges

- How much influence do children currently wield in your category? And at what ages do they wield it?
- If the current degree of kid influence in your category is small, can you shift the dynamics by developing brands that appeal more directly to a child's needs?
- And more importantly, do you know exactly what, in essence, the child's needs are?

2

Targeting a Kid's Heart
and Attaining "Ever-Cool"

The great man is he who does not lose his child's-heart.
—Mencius (372-289 B.C.)

IN MANY WAYS, the timeless needs that children strive to satisfy are not all that different from those of adults. Some are
innate; some are acquired. Children must satisfy physiological demands such as the need for food and shelter. They
strive to achieve safety and security. Children seek the social
needs of love, belonging, acceptance, appreciation, and
friendship. They attempt to fulfill their ego, which demands
self-respect and pride. Given a child's tender years, such
needs are intense, especially since children depend so much
on others to fulfill them. So children strive to be independent, capable, and in control. They need to learn, aspire,
and achieve. They need to dream many dreams.

Through the colorful prism that is the child's heart,
these needs are satisfied in many ways. And kid brands that
survive decades to become phenomenal successes do so, in
large part, because they found a path that satisfied one or
more of those needs.

"Barbie fulfills a fundamental need that all girls share,"
begins Jean McKenzie, Mattel's executive vice-president and
general manager, Worldwide Barbie, "by playing out what it
might be like in the grown-up world." Through Barbie, girls
can dream of the achievement, glamour, romance, adventure,

and nurturing opportunities that may someday be theirs. Such dreams touch upon many timeless needs, ranging from pride and success to belonging and love. Mattel zeros in on these core desires and addresses them with a different Barbie product. Barbie, for example, has been a teacher, a fashion model, a girlfriend, an astronaut, and a big sister.

Mattel then introduces new Barbie dolls every year in order to keep up-to-date with the latest definitions of achievement, glamour, romance, adventure, and nurturing. "We made Barbie a nurse in 1962 when little girls dreamed of being a nurse," says Nancy Zwiers, senior vice-president of worldwide marketing for Barbie. "Then we made Barbie a doctor years later to both reflect, and encourage, girls' broadening aspirations." Similarly, Mattel in recent years introduced such dolls as Crystal Barbie doll (a gorgeous glamour doll), Great Shape Barbie doll (thus to tie into the aerobics workout craze), Flight Time Barbie doll (a pilot), and Troll Barbie doll and Baywatch Barbie doll (to tie into kid fads and television shows).

The "Ever-Cool" Formula of Success

With Barbie, Mattel targets both the emotional needs that stay the same and the trends and fads that shift. That is how the Barbie doll stays "cool" year after year. McDonald's does the same with the Happy Meal. The Happy Meal, first tested by McDonald's in Kansas City in the late seventies, satisfies the child's desire for a tasty meal, yet it stays "current" in a large part by offering promotional tie-ins (e.g., figurines) to connect with whatever fad or movie is currently "cool" with kids (e.g., *The Little Mermaid, Hook, 101 Dalmatians*). Even the smaller, unassuming brand of PEZ Candy has been plodding comfortably forward year after year in the United States, staying contemporary by changing the shape of its candy dispenser. Since 1952, literally hundreds of variations have been introduced and have included vintage characters like Bugs Bunny as well as more contemporary characters such as Teenage Mutant Ninja Turtles and seasonal characters like Santa Claus. Always, however, PEZ satisfies the timeless sweet tooth.

Hence, successful marketers must identify and address key eternal needs, yet inject a degree of flexibility in their marketing programs via new products, promotions, or advertising that allows them to stay fresh and contemporary. That is the Ever-Cool formula, graphically demonstrated in Exhibit #2-1. Simply stated, satisfy a kid's timeless emotional need(s) but routinely dress it up in a current fad or trend, just as Mattel does with Barbie, as McDonald's does with the Happy Meal, or as PEZ Candy does with its candy containers. As trends and fads shift, simply jump to the next while continuing to target the timeless emotional need that the brand fulfills, thus never losing sight of the role the brand plays in a child's life.

If you can invent the fad, even better. Disney does this. The continuous release of new, successful films keeps Disney, the master brand, current and fresh. The movies it releases (e.g., *The Lion King*) are sub-brands whose elements are licensed to others, although each has a limited shelf life as do all fads. Disney is also a master of re-releasing older films to a new generation of viewers, thus perpetuating both the film and the fad seemingly forever.

Even long-standing brands like Play-Doh and LEGO have found it necessary to evolve to stay current. So, too, do some people. Madonna became popular among teens by emphasizing rebellion and sexuality in her music and performances. Both reflect timeless emotions. But to stay current, she must continuously re-invent herself every few years to push the boundaries of what rebellion and sexuality are. And in so doing, Madonna stays at the cutting edge of several deep-rooted emotions.

There are many fascinating ways to successfully employ the Ever-Cool formula. They will be explored throughout this book.

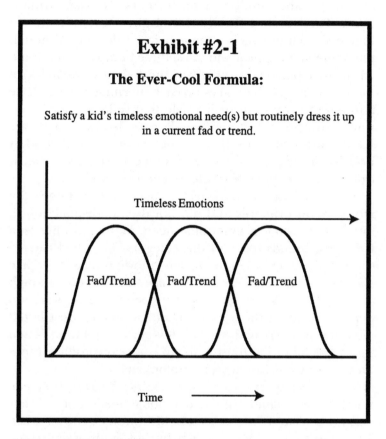

Exhibit #2-1

The Ever-Cool Formula:

Satisfy a kid's timeless emotional need(s) but routinely dress it up in a current fad or trend.

Timeless Emotions

Fad/Trend   Fad/Trend   Fad/Trend

Time

Roots of Extinction

There are three key scenarios that prevent brands from achieving longevity. First, a brand may uniquely satisfy a long-standing emotional need, but not be able to adequately update itself as trends and fads shift. Such was the case with He-Man action figures. This was a wildly successful, boy-oriented brand that fulfilled a boy's timeless need for power (see chapter 3), but it was unable to re-invent itself year after year in order to appear new again. So after a very successful run, it was eventually bumped off by a succession of other brands such as Transformers, Teenage Mutant Ninja Turtles, and finally the Mighty Morphin Power Rangers, each of which ultimately faced decline. Although phenomenal in appeal and sales, these brands are too limited in their persona to maintain the height of their initial success. When Barbie wakes up each morning, she can have a different profession or life-style that reflects a girl's current aspirations, but a Power Ranger is always a Power Ranger, just waiting for the next new craze to knock it off. A new movie might revive Power Rangers for a time, but it can be a very expensive way to extend longevity.

Secondly, some brands decline because they targeted a fad or trend primarily and did not do an adequate job of satisfying a timeless emotional need. Many past, licensed kid-cereal brands fell into this category. They had carried successful names based upon some movie or character, like *Ghostbusters*, but their taste or texture was not good enough or unique enough to entice a loyal customer. They were too dependent upon the appeal of the fad alone. Most lasted eighteen months or less. The lesson: every brand based upon a trend or fad must first have superior product attributes of its own before it seeks prolonged life.

Thirdly, some brands become extinct because they neither satisfied a child's innate emotional needs, nor did they tie into the latest fads or trends. Most never get to market. The ones that do, typically get buried by the retail trade within a year due to lackluster sales.

Some of the above scenarios can be quite profitable in the short term. Some manufacturers, for example, will develop a brand based upon a fad, knowing full well that its life is short. They manage the birth, growth, and eventual extinction of the brand by promoting it until the fad wanes, while not sinking too many resources into it. These brands never become Ever-Cools because they were never meant to be. Smart thinking, perhaps, but far smaller profits than what an Ever-Cool can provide.

Although many examples of both Ever-Cools and not will be cited throughout this book, the ultimate goal is to help the kid marketer understand both the "timeless" and the "shifting" in hopes that it will help him create and sustain an enduring kid brand, one that is immune to extinction.

Fun Defined

Fun is best defined as emotional needs satisfied. It can be achieved, for instance, by fulfilling a boy's desire to attain power or by satisfying a girl's search for glamour, each of which fulfills a timeless dream that gives way to feelings of pride and accomplishment. Unfortunately, the word *fun* is the most overused, misunderstood, dangerous word in the kid kingdom. Too many marketers generally advise that kid products, advertising, or promotions should be fun, but add very little knowledge as to what fun actually means. Without that knowledge, people search randomly for fun as though it were the Holy Grail; they hope to recognize it when they see it.

Barbara Lui, creative director with Ogilvy & Mather on the Mattel business, was once asked to make a certain commercial *fun*. She paused, smiled, and then asked politely, "Of course it will be fun, but what *kind of* fun do you have in mind?" That question, and its ultimate answer, is at the very heart of every successful marketing plan that aims to excite a child.

The dimensions of this *fun* are as vast as a child's needs. It takes on many faces, has many guises. Its origin lies in the very psyche of the child, in a place that is as ancient and as timeless as mankind, where childhood's emotional needs abound, waiting to be satisfied. Children go there often. Most adults have forgotten the path. Any kid marketer who desires success must find the way.

The path to the child's psyche, to his heart, begins here. Now. But you must first cast aside your adult worries and responsibilities, let down the defenses you have created and maintained throughout the years, and once again connect yourself to the child that dwells within your soul.

Brand Challenges

- Are you applying the Ever-Cool formula?
- Can you identify the timeless, emotional need(s) that your current brand satisfies?
- Do you really know which aspects of *fun* your brand touches?
- What is the overall plan for ensuring that your brand will remain "current" year after year?

PART II
The Child's Psyche

The Child's Psyche

The term *psyche* has its roots in Greek mythology and once referred to a maiden who was loved by Eros and eventually became the personification of the soul. Handed down through the ages, *psyche* is now a term used to denote that part of each of us that governs our thoughts and feelings, both consciously and subconsciously. It is the intangible, yet ever-present entity that shapes what we think, how we behave, what we dream. It is, when all is said and done, who we are.

And while children cannot describe the essence of their own, evolving psyche (nor can adults for that matter), children do give us clues in the things they love and in the things they hate. It bubbles on the surface like an amusing brew of a delightful potion. For brief moments, and only if you look closely enough, you can catch a glimpse of a child's precious, emotionally-laden psyche. You can witness the many dimensions of fun, which reflect the needs satisfied, and use such knowledge to launch new brands and rejuvenate existing ones.

Part II will begin your journey to the better understanding of the timeless truths that dwell deep within children everywhere. It begins with a peek into the psyche of both boys (chapter 3) and girls (chapter 4), for many of the most enduring Ever-Cools fulfill gender-specific needs, ones that are pervasive. This part of the book then delves into the many things the genders share such as their desire to conquer fear (chapter 5), their search for control (chapter 6), their preoccupation with fantasy (chapter 7), and the delight their own senses can bring (chapter 8). This section concludes with a review of how a child's psyche evolves as he gets older (chapter 9) and how reference groups help shape a child's perception of *cool* (chapter 10).

Throughout this exploration, we will examine how marketers have utilized this knowledge to develop brands that created a relationship with the child by fulfilling emotional needs. Some such brands have become Ever-Cools.

3

Touch the Boy's Psyche

Of all the animals, the boy is the most unmanageable.
—Plato (428-348 B.C.)

A BOY'S PSYCHE IS AMAZING TO BEHOLD. He can be an angel one moment and a scoundrel the next. It is his way. There will be boogers at mealtime, finger paints on the walls, and the desire to beat his dear old dad at virtually any and all tests of strength or intelligence.

A girl's psyche will share many such elements explained throughout this chapter, but will often manifest itself in far different ways, to be explained in chapter 4. How many of these differences are innate versus the result of socialization, I will leave for sociologists to figure out—but such differences are real and tangible.

Getting in touch with the boy's psyche is crucial. To help prepare for the film *Jack*, Robin Williams and Francis Ford Coppola went camping with a bunch of ten-year-old boys to help them remember what it was like to be that age. They spent two weeks playing games, fishing, and camping. They ate peanut butter and jelly sandwiches and had food fights—the works. They were in search of memories. Afterwards, they made the film. This demonstrates the importance of understanding your audience and the lengths people will go to achieve it.

What follows is not a complete summary of a boy's

psyche, just those aspects that tend to manifest themselves in the fun of emotional needs fulfilled.

POWER: *The ability or capacity to act or perform effectively*

When I was in grade school, I made it a point to arrive fifteen minutes before the first bell rang. The purpose was to match my skills against the other boys in what was referred to simply as *the race.* Dozens of us would bunch up at a fence at one end of the school yard, and at the designated shout from a school chum, we would race to the opposite fence. The winner got the applause, the attention, the admiration for running his fastest and beating the rest. In short, it was pride—a strong emotional benefit—derived from the feeling of power that came from strong limbs, a swift gait, and strength purified. The winner felt like the god Hermes, no less, with sandals fitted with wings. Or, in our case, with tennis shoes known as PF Flyers, whose advertising claimed the shoes would help us run faster and jump higher. It must have been successful for its time, as sales of PF Flyers reached $100 million at the height of its popularity around the early 1970s.

Boys gravitate toward endeavors that best tell the world that power is theirs. Sports can do that, whether that be blasting a ball over a fence, gliding it into a hoop, or powering it into the end zone. It can also come from performing on a high bar—twisting and turning, releasing and spinning, and dismounting. The feeling of power can come from involvement in the martial arts and the confidence that sport can instill. Power is also derived from intelligence—a score on a test; a correct answer given in class; the ability to out-think, out-strategize, out-smart.

Boys are continuously in search for such icons of power each and every day. It is very much a part of who they are and how they define themselves. The ancient Greeks understood this and imbued their gods with power. Zeus, lord of the sky, wielded the thunderbolt. Hermes was the swiftest with winged sandals. Apollo was the archer-god, master musician, and healer. And then there was Hercules, the greatest of all Greek heroes—strong, brave, confident. These qualities are the aspiration of all boys, no matter what the age.

Many marketers have associated their brands with some form of power and have achieved wonderful results. Gatorade is one such brand, and it has become a standard at many kid sporting events. The label on a packet of Gatorade reads "delivers the fluids, electrolytes and carbohydrate energy that your body needs for peak performance." The key power words are *energy* and *peak performance,* and they are served up with concrete proof—*fluids, electrolytes, carbohydrate.* It is the number-one sports drink. The Nike brand has a power derived from attitude—"Just do it." In fact, the first Olympic chant of the modern era was "Nike! Nike!" *Nike,* it seems, is the Greek word for "victory." The Mighty Morphin Power Rangers wield their power via the martial arts and use it to vanquish evil. In fact, from Superman to the Terminator, wielding power has been a central goal—one that boys desire to achieve.

One brand stands above the rest year after year in associating itself with physical fitness, implied power, and the sports-related achievement that can come from it. It is not necessarily for just kids, per se, but for the kid in all of us. Introduced in 1924 by General Mills, Wheaties soon became the Breakfast of Champions, a claim that hints of power derived from a healthy breakfast and athletic prowess. Wheaties' first sponsorship of sports was associated with play-by-play radio baseball broadcasts in 1933, which was also the year "the Breakfast of Champions" slogan was first used. Athlete testimonials were a key part of the marketing approach. In the early years, Wheaties was endorsed by the likes of Babe Ruth, Joe DiMaggio, Ted Williams, and Mickey Mantle. The first athlete to appear nationally on a box of Wheaties was Bob Richards, two-time Olympic pole-vaulting champion.

Wheaties and its athletes have become so much a part of our culture that during the 1996 Olympics, the press openly speculated about which athletes General Mills would pick to represent the virtues of today's champion. Those picked would have the honor to adorn the box of Wheaties itself. In fact, one report stated that General Mills hoped to see Wheaties sales jump as much as 20 percent as a result of the 1996 Olympics.

In this way, Wheaties has captured the winning Ever-Cool formula. The brand appeals to a timeless emotional need (i.e., physical fitness/power), and then routinely defines it in today's terms (i.e., the celebrity champion). And it works. Wheaties is a well-established brand that stays current and successful year after year.

It is amazing to think that during the 1950s, Wheaties actually abandoned sports to go after the so-called "kids" market by associating itself with the Lone Ranger and the Mickey Mouse Club. The cereal maker gained more kids, but lost too many adults. They went back to their sports roots and captured the kid in many of us, young and old. Wheaties is an Ever-Cool.

GOOD VERSUS EVIL: *the positive, the moral versus the bad, the wicked*

Boys, so say sociologists, are simply more aggressive than are girls. And good versus evil is one way it manifests itself. So boys will, at times, desire strength and power in order to vanish some real or imaginary evil foe. This basic good-versus-evil storyline is taught to boys in both subtle and overt ways: God versus Satan, David versus Goliath, Jack versus the Giant. The storyteller's purpose was to convey a sense of right and wrong, of morality, of codes of conduct. Many parents tell their children that when evil cannot be averted or converted with reason, then force is a possible, although last, resort. Such force may include power, strength, cleverness, intelligence, agility, or speed.

All of these are enticements to a boy, who through countless centuries was called upon to defend nations and homesteads and families from those who would destroy them.

And even in countries today that live in relative peace, a boy's nature cannot be subdued. He will play good versus evil. He will fantasize about defending the universe if need be, thus satisfying an emotional need given to him at birth and nurtured by society. Still, many parents, this one included, will be concerned when their child plays out a good versus evil story in overly violent ways. This will be further discussed in chapter 19.

But of all the brands that have come and gone, only a few have withstood the test of time, vanquished evil again and again to the delight of kids, and won the acceptance of many parents. The G.I. Joe brand is one of them. Why? Because he represents not only strength, not only good overcoming evil, but also our nation's real defense against all evil challengers big and small. So as evils spring up in the real world, boys imagine that they can defend their country from it, and G.I. Joe is the conduit through which they can fantasize. He is a boy's Barbie doll. Sure, the Mighty Morphin Power Rangers or Teenage Mutant Ninja Turtles, or the Transformers before them, or even He-Man before that, could come to our nation's aid. But they are fads. G.I. Joe figures are here to stay because their play pattern is real enough for all boys to imagine that they are, in truth, G.I. Joe. Significantly, G.I. Joe stays contemporary by introducing updated themes and new "recruits." In 1993, for example, we saw the introduction of a Star Brigade (space) version and a Ninja Force (martial arts) G.I. Joe, among others. In fact, there have been more than 230 different G.I. Joe figures introduced since 1964. And they have equated to more than $2.6 billion, comprised of more than 300 million soldier figures and some 200 million vehicles (1994 estimates). Hasbro uses G.I. Joe to satisfy an eternal emotion, yet constantly updates him to be relevant in today's world. G.I. Joe is an Ever-Cool.

GROSS: *Coarse, vulgar, offensive, disgusting*

In many seminars I have given to marketers, I will often introduce my audience to some rather interesting boys' products. Nothing gets as much amusement as those products that stray to the gross and bizarre side of a young boy's psyche. There is one particular demonstration that I love to give. Sometimes I do it with a product known as S.N.O.T., which stands for Super Nauseating Obnoxious Treat. It is a slimy, green, liquid candy in a clear, plastic container resembling a human nose. When the nose plugs are removed, the candy slides down through the nasal cavity and onto your finger; and then you, the eight-year-old boy, eat it. In my typical demonstration, I select a volunteer from the audience and ask him politely if he would be kind enough to try a product. With a smile he always agrees, and then I pull S.N.O.T from my bag and watch him squirm. As I squeeze a long drip of the product out of the nasal cavity and onto his finger, the crowd around him starts to laugh, and the volunteer's smile fades to disbelief and then to disgust. He is trapped and he knows it. As he reluctantly tastes it, the crowd howls. Then I ask him how it tasted. The relieved response is typically, "Well . . . fine . . . just sweet."

However, the taste is not the key benefit at all. The key benefit was the howls, the laughs, the attention I sparked when I surprised the volunteer with S.N.O.T. That was the real treat. I was able to be gross and received admiration from those around me—really cool. For somewhere buried deep within the boy's psyche there is a little section with a gross label on it, and every boy goes there often. Still, S.N.O.T. may remain just a forgotten novelty unless its manufacturers can find a way to keep it current each year.

Gross *sells* in many arenas. Nickelodeon and Mattel introduced Gak, a purple goo, inspired by an unruly Nickelodeon

program, "Double Dare." Eight million units were reportedly sold in 1993 alone. There is also a book entitled *Gross Grub*
by Cheryl Porter, which boasts of "wretched recipes that look
yucky but taste yummy." Such great recipes include Boogers-
on-a-Stick and Butchered Snake Bits with Barbecue Sauce.
Serving such fare is bound to make a boy the center of attention at his tenth birthday party. That is the real benefit. I can
easily foresee updated revisions of the book with recipes that
continue to explore the gross arena, thus allowing her book
to be continuously refreshed. She touched a timeless emotion in a medium that allows her to stay current as fads and
trends shift.

The Ever-Cool award may, in the long run, go to
Nickelodeon's "Ren & Stimpy," a cartoon about a
Chihuahua and a plump, gullible feline who find a bizarre
friendship. They continue to push the envelope of what is
considered gross and bizarre. In fact, they will go to great
lengths for a joke. In one episode, Stimpy expels gas, which
takes on a live, ghostly appearance. Stimpy then falls in love
with it. I will leave the details to your imagination. My wife
was repulsed when we saw the episode. My son, however,
fell to the floor laughing and loved it all the more because
his mother was "grossed out."

SILLINESS: *Frivolous*

The funny bone, what a marvelous thing it is. And while
"funny bone" connotes a physical object, the real funny
bone is mental, buried deep within the heart of a boy; yet it
is ready at a moment's notice to explode him into laughs,
giggles, and howls. The sillier and more outrageous the
prank, stunt, joke, or facial expression, the more we can see
this part of a boy's psyche.

Physical humor falls into this category. Witnessing someone slip on a banana peel still makes a boy fall to the floor
with laughter. A pie in the face accomplishes the same
response. Marketers in many categories have targeted this

part of the psyche well. Watching the dazed and bewildered Wile E. Coyote just miss catching the Road Runner before falling off a mile-high cliff, punching through low-lying clouds, and finally smacking headfirst into the rock-hard surface of the desert is a real crowd pleaser; we especially love that puff of dust that rises when he hits. It is silly, physical humor, not unlike *The Three Stooges* films many of us grew up watching. Nickelodeon is a master of the silly, among other things. In their show "What Would You Do?" adults commonly get hit with a pie in the face. It is always fun to see someone else a victim of such a situation.

Whereas girls will get a laugh from such antics and then stop, boys will continue to roll on the floor in hysterics. They will even play back the episode time and again and tell it to their friends; they will pass it along endlessly. A girl will just roll her eyes and shake her head as he continues. "Stop being so stupid," she will say. "It wasn't *that* funny." Yet for him it was!

And that silly Trix Rabbit just cannot seem to get those Trix no matter what lengths he goes to. "Silly rabbit," the kids might retort. "Trix are for kids!" The brand's advertising, among other things, keeps it contemporary by finding new ways for that silly rabbit to obtain the Trix, only to be foiled once again. It is an Ever-Cool scenario, in this case appealing to boys and girls alike.

BRAVERY: *Possessing or displaying courage*

I came home from work one day and was greeted by my son, Matt, at the door. He was excited.

"Gotta see this," he said while kneeling down to roll up his pant leg. And there, reddened and scraped and oozing, was a huge gash on his knee. As I bent over, concern flooding my face, I asked him if he was OK. He responded with a broad smile and eager pride, "Fine, Dad. Isn't it cool?" Matt proceeded to tell me how he tried to do a trick on his bike only to take a big spill.

"Didn't it hurt?" I asked.

"Just a little," he said, before running outside as his friends passed the house. He was intent upon showing them his wound. Perhaps it was really a badge of courage.

Matt had taken a big spill that day. My wife told me afterwards that he came home crying, his eyes swollen, his nerves unglued. But as he calmed down, and after he realized he had survived a treacherous fate and lived to tell the tale, his fear turned to pride. He saw himself as tough. He had gazed into the evil eyes of terror and had survived, and that was cool.

Boys like the feeling of bravery that can come from testing their nerve against some hurdle, whether that be a force of nature, a force of wills, or a force of circumstance. Such controlled, safe, although implied danger, is fun for boys. Driving a race car is considered dangerous; by driving a go-cart, a boy can feel that he, too, is stretching the limits of safety but in a relatively harmless way. The wind in his hair, the bends of the track, the loud roar of a small engine, the "potential" to crash up. That is bravery!

Some brands have targeted a boy's desire to take a risk, to be brave, to beat danger. One soft drink called KICK, a citrus soda bottled by Seven-Up/RC Bottling Company, has a warning on the can that reads, "Warning: Contains stuff you don't even want to know about!" And "May be too intense for some members of the general public." What a delicious danger it implies. Another is a novelty candy called Busted!, manufactured in Canada for a company called Leaf. It is a bag with ten gum balls that declares "Warning! Three gumballs are way hot! And I double dog dare ya to find out which three!!" MEGA WARHEADS are sour hard candies that come with a caution: "First 50 seconds are EXTREMELY INTENSE! Hang in there!" The back of the bag has a chart that rates how brave you are based upon how long you kept this very sour treat in your mouth. All these novelties offer a touch of a challenge, an ounce of harmless danger, and a ton of fun. Are these brands fads or Ever-Cools? They are possibly the former unless marketers can discover ways to keep them contemporary.

TO SUCCEED/TO MASTER: *The desired result, the skilled*

Many of the emotions cited thus far are interrelated. At the root of many of them is a boy's desire to be the best he can be, to achieve, to feel competent. Mom and Dad tell him to do well in school; to learn; and to excel at sports, art, or whatever. He understands the notion of getting better with practice, of achieving some noble goal, and of racing headfirst toward some real or imagined finish line.

A boy must achieve! There is nothing like the thrill that comes from being first that pushes him to achieve. It is part power, as cited earlier, but also part inner pride. And there is also the desire to win approval from those who witness the glory. That is why many commercials for board games end in the same timeless phrase, "I win!" In fact, look all around a kid's world and you'll find that the desire to win is pervasive. Go into Chuck E. Cheese's and witness the games that dispense tickets a child can win that are redeemable for prizes. See the long stream of tickets the boy will clutch in his fist, hang about his neck, or stuff in his pockets; these are all a badge declaring he is a winner. Visit the cereal aisle of your neighborhood supermarket and watch as the boy picks up every box, then turns it about to see what prize he can win by sending in box tops. Go to the school yard and watch the face of the boy who comes in first in a noble race, or feel the triumph of the eight-year-old when he makes a game-winning basket from ten feet out. You will see competence displayed.

Yet winning is a tricky thing. If it is too easy to win, the boy gets bored. If it is too hard, the boy gets defeated too often, loses interest, and looks for another place or activity in which he can succeed. The goal, then, is to create a game that is challenging but possible. Videogame software developers know this too well. That is why the best games have multiple levels. The game allows the boy to feel like a winner when he beats (survives) the first level, yet still gives him the challenge of plenty more levels. This is a very small insight, but a rather brilliant one, indeed.

Mastery takes the form of constructing, of building, of creating and the pride that it engenders. Tinkertoys, Erector Sets, and LEGO come immediately to mind. Each allows a boy to use his imagination to construct a world, neighborhood, or car as he sees it. He can then sit back and say with pride "I did that," which creates a strong emotional response. The LEGO brand is of particular interest. The word LEGO is formed from the Danish words "LEg GOdt" meaning "play well." In Latin, the word means "I study," and "I put together." Evolving for many decades, the LEGO brand was extended into a huge array of sets and themes (e.g., trains, pirates, ships, castles, underwater, etc.) that touch different parts of a boy's interests and psyche (and a girl's, too), although in a contemporary way that can be updated as interests change. In fact, some 110 billion LEGO elements were molded from 1949 to 1990. Few brands in the world approach the magnitude of LEGO.

LOVE: *Intense affection*

A younger boy, say younger than four years, is open and free with his affection. "I love you, Mommy," is a common phrase. Warm hugs at nighttime, a kiss good morning, even a Cabbage Patch Kids doll under a Christmas tree is A-OK. It is a need to give and receive love, a need to be needed. The love and affection bubbles near the surface when a boy is younger, and it is a dear comfort to Mom and Dad alike.

Then things change. One day, little Johnny does not kiss Mom back or little Michael no longer reaches for Dad's hand at the store. The boy may be age five or six now and has friends at school who will readily accuse him of being *babyish* if they see him being kissed by his mom. After all, the boy wants power now. He is supposed to win the race. He gets extra points for grossing out girls.

One three-year-old boy loved his Cabbage Patch Kids doll dearly and slept with him every night for years. The doll's name was Rusty. Years later, Rusty was gone from sight, stuck at the back of the boy's closet for none to see, because the boy was now nine. Then came an embarrassing moment when Rusty came into view at an inappropriate time when his nine-year-old friends, all boys, were about. "And who's this?" asked one of the lads with a smirk. After fidgeting with embarrassment and hoping to save face, the doll's owner replied, "T-Rex!"

Make no mistake, a nine-year-old boy still needs to give and receive plenty of affection. But such a display cannot be as overt as it was in the past. A boy might slug his father on the arm as he passes him to the bathroom. That is love. Or he might save some popcorn for his mom, who had none. That is display of love, too. Or, just maybe, he might surprise her with a big, but quick hug when no one is watching. Family games help provide a connection from boy to parents, as do organized sports. But brands can provide a connection, too. Few of my generation can forget the commercials that depicted a boy and his dad sharing a LIFESAVERS candy. The brand became a conduit of affection between parent and child; it was really well done.

Nickelodeon's program "Doug" is about a friendly, good-hearted, average kid who, when confronted by life's average hurdles, always seems to find the right path. There is a lot of nurturing and learning there; that makes it hard to believe that the same young boy who watches "Doug" will also tune in to "Ren & Stimpy," which pushes the boundaries of gross and bizarre. It is the same kid, with just a different part of his psyche needing to be tickled.

Steven Spielberg touched a nurturing part of a boy's soul, and everyone else's, with *E.T. The Extra-Terrestrial.*

Instead of creating a scary extra-terrestrial bent upon destroying the earth, we find, instead, an affable, caring, huggable one who eventually weakens to the point of death and must rely on a boy to nurture him, defend him, and save him. It is nurturing, but in a heroic way and at an exhilarating pace—just how a boy might love it! The film became one of the biggest box-office hits of all time, grossing more than $700 million worldwide.

Brand Challenges

- Is your brand the best at touching a boy's psyche in one or more ways? Does it or can it help him be or feel
  - powerful?
  - like the protector of good?
  - gross?
  - silly?
  - brave?
  - like a winner?
  - nurturing, but in a boy-acceptable way?

4

Touch the Girl's Psyche

Beautiful, golden goddess . . . The breath of the west wind bore her . . .
—"Homeric Hymn of the Goddess Aphrodite"

I WALKED MY PRECIOUS FIVE-YEAR-OLD DAUGHTER to school on her first day of kindergarten. The sun was shining. The cool morning breeze was caressing her soft, pink cheeks, and the sounds of a hundred children's voices punctuated the air as she stood in line. She waited patiently for the morning bell to ring and for her first teacher to open the first door to a new and expanding world.

I stood there, just gazing at her posture; she stood so straight. Her hands were clasped so delicately before her. Her pretty velvet dress was gorgeous, as was her well-groomed hair. Megan had spent a good amount of time preparing herself that morning—just the right dress, just the right hair style, just the right barrettes. And the other girls in line looked the same: groomed, delicate, calm, and polite as they each stood there, straight and tall and orderly.

This was quite a contrast to the mangled line of boys next to them. The boys' mischievous souls could not be hidden by the freshly painted coat of new clothes. Several were pushing each other, each trying to become the line leader. Others were tapping the backs of their classmates two spots ahead of them and then turning abruptly away

before they got caught. They were loud, silly, obnoxious urchins. Their frustrated parents desperately tried to corral the brood.

Now, any parent of one of the girls could mistakenly believe that he simply had better parenting skills. Sure, that explains why the boys were a bit out of control. The boys' parents must not have read all those books on child upbringing. Wrong! Having brought my own son to his first day of kindergarten a few years earlier, I knew that the difference in behavior exhibited in these two lines at kindergarten had far less to do with parenting skills and far more to do with both genetics and deeply rooted social mores. Yes, girls can be challenging, and their psyche shares a lot of common ground with that of boys. But a girl seeks emotional fulfillment in distinctly different ways.

BEAUTY: *A pleasing quality associated with the quality of form or color or excellence of craftsmanship*

At focus groups some years ago, I watched from behind a one-way mirror while five- and six-year-old girls tried on cosmetics designed specifically for them. The excitement they expressed even upon learning the reason for the research was telling. There were "oohs" and giggles all around as lip gloss was passed from tiny fingers to tiny fingers around the room. Then, spontaneously, the eight little girls in each group dashed to the mirror and began to apply various colors and shades of lip gloss. Gazing into that mirror, they were looking right at us but could not see us gazing back. And what a sight it was. With lips curled and eyes squinting in concentration, they applied the lip gloss as expertly as five- and six-year-old fingers might. Their eyes told us that they cared much about this craft. Later in the group, in fact, they would each recount how they watched their own mothers as they applied adult brands and hoped for the day when they could as well. Many of the girls admitted that their mothers had already let them wear makeup (mostly a very light lipstick) and that it made them feel very grown-up. All children have this emotional need to feel grown-up. It is manifested here in a girl's desire to be pretty.

By age five, girls understand that beauty is a craft and most of them are already an apprentice under the care and guidance of their mothers. I am always amazed that marketers are often faulted for placing too much emphasis on beauty when, in fact, such attitudes are reinforced at such an early age in the home. As a mother strives to achieve beauty, so will her daughter, who wants desperately to be just like her hero—Mom.

So, little girls strive for beauty in all its forms: the clothes they wear, the way they fix their hair, their shoes, their socks, and all. The cosmetics they apply become more important as they get older, as does the perfume they wear. Girls simply want to look and feel the best they can in the eyes of their friends and parents. Later in life they seek the approval of boyfriends, but most importantly, they want to look and feel the best they can for themselves.

Boys may be into power, but girls have the market cornered on beauty, and marketers know it. Candy manufacturers have adorned little girls with candy necklaces, bracelets, and more recently, with candy rings. Even makers of bandages seem to realize that if the bandage has a pretty image on it, girls will wear it whether or not they have a cut or scrape. (Boys will, too, but they prefer a different type of image).

Chief among the beauty makers is Tinkerbell cosmetics. In 1952, Tom Fields, LTD., registered the Tinkerbell trademark for a wide range of toiletries and related categories. After that, millions of girls were allowed to feel just a bit older, just a bit more feminine and more beautiful—all very powerful emotional needs. Tinkerbell has become a small rite of passage, for it plays a role in a young girl's life by satisfying those needs. And in so doing, the Tinkerbell line now sells more than eight million units annually. It is marketed in some seventy-eight countries around the world and has been a favorite across four generations of young women. Importantly, it has managed to freshen itself via new products and packaging and such to remain a contemporary, Ever-Cool part of a younger girl's life.

This desire for beauty also spills over into their artistic side in the crafts girls make, the things they draw, in the works of art they mold or paint. Girls express themselves through the beauty they create. There is pride in that, too, the "look what I did" appeal.

GLAMOUR: *An air of compelling charm, romance, and excitement*

While beauty is only skin deep, glamour is something else all together. Glamour is really about excitement, and you don't have to be beautiful to be glamorous. It is the charm that matters, that feeling of romance, the thrill of leading an exciting life.

Many adults do not really understand the Barbie brand. They see her only as a beautiful shell, or worse, as an icon of all that is wrong with society because she presumably overemphasizes an unrealistic, unattainable beauty. That is an adult talking, coming from either a man who never understood the magic of Barbie or from a woman who has forgotten what Barbie meant to her so long ago.

Yes, Barbie is beautiful; but at the heart of it all, Barbie is really about glamour. Barbie leads a romantic, exciting, fun-loving life. And through Barbie dolls, little girls fantasize of a life that they, too, might lead some day. Barbie is independent, her own person, and not the least bit dependent on Ken. Barbie was an astronaut. She was a doctor. She was queen of the ball. She has been a stewardess and a pilot. She has been a gold medalist in the Olympics. And why not? Barbie aspires to be the best she can be at volleyball, at scuba diving, whatever little girls aspire to be in today's world. That is the Ever-Cool formula: timeless emotions satisfied in a contemporary way. And Barbie has a whole world that unfolds before a girl's eyes of jet planes and a comfortable home, a nice car, and plenty of family and friends.

As one eight-year-old told me not so long ago, "Barbie is so real she doesn't know she's just a doll." That is right. Mattel has applied the Ever-Cool formula so aptly that Barbie has developed a *persona* that girls relate to. And Barbie touches so many aspects of a girl's psyche from adventure to independence to dreams of aspirations, that the emotional connections with the Barbie brand run deep. Find a seven-year-old girl a hundred years from now and ask her what is cool. Providing the caretakers of the Barbie brand continue to apply the Ever-Cool formula, the little girl's answer will be "Barbie!"

MOTHERING: *The qualities characteristic of a mother, as in maternal affection*

Somewhere deep within the heart of a girl there exists an emotional foundation that needs to express a gentle, mothering persona. Certainly much of it is innate, but a lot is also acquired as little girls watch their own mothers and others care for younger children. It is a deep-rooted need to give and receive love. It is a need to be needed.

Girls just love to play mom. They will do so with younger siblings, with their baby doll, and in the absence of that, with their pet dog, cat, or hamster—whatever is handy. This innate drive has made many a brand successful. One of the greatest successes in marketing memory is the Cabbage Patch Kids doll.

In Cabbage Patch Kids, girls found a rather pudgy-looking baby just yearning to be loved, with outstretched arms waiting for a loving embrace from its adoptive parent. The soft, squishy body, the snub-nosed face, the quality detail of a newborn, the birth certificate, the adoption papers, the heart-wrenching appeal of a baby without a home, the one-of-a-kind appeal—all of these things said love me, hold me, adopt me. From the marketer's perspective, they said *buy me!* At the peak of the Cabbage Patch Kids doll success in 1985, sales were reported at $600 million.

It proved that the closer marketers can get to creating the mothering experience, the more they could touch the heart of the child, all compliments of Xavier Roberts, creator of the Cabbage Patch Kids doll. Of particularly interest was the fact that the Cabbage Patch Kids doll was introduced in an age of "do-something" baby dolls that would burp or pee or eat or talk or whatever. Cabbage Patch Kids dolls had no technology, but they out-sold everything that did. Emotion, in its pure form, is significantly more powerful than batteries. Dr. Paul Horton, author of *Solace,* a study of humans' need for objects to give comfort, told the *New York Times* in 1984 that children "need attachments external to themselves to give solace and comfort" and that a Cabbage Patch Kid doll "is a possession a child is instantly able to make his own."

But the brand struggled in subsequent years because no one was able to find ways to make the brand truly "new" again. Sales in 1986 had dropped to $230 million. Attempts to contemporize it, even to add a talking feature, could not bring the Cabbage Patch Kids doll back to its top sales performance. The addition of a chewing feature even drew complaints when a few children claimed that the doll chewed their hair. So Cabbage Patch Kids dolls have declined to a lower sales plateau, although the brand remains on the market today as probably one of the best-ever attempts to touch the mothering part of a girl's psyche.

Pound Puppies plush toys took the basic nurturing and adoption concept of Cabbage Patch Kids dolls, applied it to a plush animal, and was very successful. "Rescuing a puppy or kitten from the pound and making it your own is a very strong emotional play pattern for a child," says Scott Masline, vice-president of marketing for Lewis Galoob Toys, Inc. It developed into a very compelling, nurturing brand idea.

To touch a girl's nurturing instinct, Mattel introduced

The Heart Family, a line of fashion dolls that came with Mom, Dad, and a toddler boy and girl. The name said love. The family unit was complete, and it provided girls everywhere with endless nurturing fantasies. It did quite well although it eventually declined. But Mattel went on to develop a stream of new brand ideas that freshly satisfied a girl's desire to nurture. This is oftentimes the best solution when faced with a struggling, declining brand that is difficult to "freshen." Instead of throwing more money at it in order to make it appear "new again," it can be more profitable to introduce a new brand that takes a whole new approach. The manufacturing process can be one of innovation, obsolescence, innovation. That is how toy manufacturers survive year after year as they search for an Ever-Cool.

But nurturing does not have to end with toys. In Disney's *Beauty and the Beast,* our heroine, Belle, was able to see the kindness in the Beast that everyone else had missed. Finally, she fell in love with the monster, thus unleashing the prince who was held captive within. There was nurturing in her sensitivity. Girls loved that. Boys undoubtedly cared more about the battle scenes. It became the first animated film ever to be nominated for an Academy Award for Best Picture. Disney's *101 Dalmatians* puts poor little puppies at risk of landing in the hands of evil Cruella De Vil, but they are all saved in the end to the resounding delight of little girls (and boys who love any chance to vanquish evil). Puppies are merely babies with more hair and a cold, wet nose.

The Baby-sitters Club book series wins the Ever-Cool award for its many nurturing, supportive appeals. This book series tackles such contemporary topics as divorced parents, remarriages, the loss of a parent's job, a girl with diabetes, as well as the more traditional issues of boys and friendships. And each issue is experienced, addressed, and overcome. It appeals to many aspects of a girl's heart, all served up in a contemporary fashion. One source estimated that more than 125 million copies of the books have been sold since 1986.

SILLINESS: *Frivolous*

Girls can be silly, too, just as boys can. But they express silliness in vastly different ways. Whereas boys look for silliness in physical forms (there is nothing like tripping a friend on the way to school), girls will more often find silliness in social arenas. Watching parents kiss will make a young girl giggle. It will make a young boy nauseous. Girls will spend time talking on the playground, huddled in a group, laughing about the clumsiness of boys, about the clothes the other girls are wearing, about the dorkiness of their teachers.

Many times girls and boys define silliness similarly. Nickelodeon's "Wild & Crazy Kids" targets the funny bone in girls and boys alike. It is a constant stream of zany stunts. Kids and dentists will race to brush a giant-sized molar. Human bowling games are played in which kids bounce around in inner tubes. Plenty of crazy relay races and obstacle courses are commonplace. The show is very silly, but very fun for boys and girls.

TO SUCCEED/TO MASTER: *The desired result, the skilled*

Once in a couple of decades, we discover that something everyone thought was nature turns out to be nurture, or vice versa. Through the 1950s and 1960s, little girls were taught to be, well, little girls. Pretty dresses, tea parties, ballet classes, more pretty dresses. They were expected only to master the arts, whether that be in music, painting, crafts, or performing. They excelled and continue to do so. But they were taught not to compete too much, especially in physical ways, for being too competitive was not ladylike. So, they were not encouraged to play baseball, football, soccer, or any other sport that may have required contact, speed, strength, or the like. No post-World War II mother wanted her daughter to be called a *tomboy*, that designation given in years past to a class of little girls who could hit a fast ball or slide successfully into third base. Nurture required that little girls stayed free of dirt, grime, and sweat.

Then something marvelous happened. Those little girls of the 1950s and 1960s grew up. They were the baby boomers who questioned convention in all its forms and have continued to change every institution that they have touched. They plunged into colleges in unprecedented numbers. They became doctors, lawyers, and business executives. They balanced their professional aspirations with raising a family. As little girls they were expected to wear a dress, but as women they could wear what they wanted. Convention broke down, and they were the ones who shattered it. Baby boomers just did not see the need to continue the "little girls wear pink and little boys get blue" routine. If little Nancy wanted to play ball, baby boomer Mom was going to see to it that her Nancy played ball. According to the numbers, Nancy did. Almost 200,000 girls played organized soccer in the United States in 1996, according to the American Youth Soccer Organization. In fact, kids playing soccer are now a 60 to 40 ratio, boys to girls. Girls want to compete. They love to win in both physical and nonphysical endeavors. They do both to satisfy such emotional needs as accomplishment, mastery, and pride.

Nature was hidden by nurture. The Greeks understood this better than we, or why else would they have worshipped Athena, a battle-goddess, or Artemis, the huntswoman of the gods? Although both could do battle, they were each nurturing as well. They presented a full persona. A survey by Ocean Spray's Wave program reported that women who participate in athletics are considered by high schoolers to be both cool and feminine. In fact, one out of three girls plays a high school sport, according to the Women's Sports

Foundation. Make no mistake, girls are tough competitors. Coed teams are commonplace for kids even in grade school. The age of the tomboy is dead.

Marketers who have recognized this fact have successfully tapped into this precious part of a girl's soul. Nickelodeon helped lead the way with its introduction of a program called "GUTS." In it, three kids compete via tough, sometimes radical athletic events in an 18,000-square-foot arena to determine who is the toughest competitor. It takes guts to compete and more guts to win. What is most impressive about "GUTS" is that the great kid athletes compete head to head, regardless of gender. So it is very common to see boys and girls battling each other through a series of physical obstacles to determine who has the greater skill and, hence, the most guts. Nickelodeon also introduced "The Secret World of Alex Mack," the exploits of a girl who obtained special powers when she was accidentally doused with a top-secret experimental compound. Alex can turn herself into a liquid or shoot balls of electricity out of her hands. She can also control the movement of people and objects by generating a magnetic field. And yet, she is a rather average kid who uses her secret, super powers to help her through everyday challenges that face her in junior high school.

Appreciating a strong, female lead is not really a recent phenomenon. It is just becoming more consistent. None of us can forget Mary Poppins and her magical powers to do good or Dorothy and her battle with the Wicked Witch of the West.

Wheaties recognizes a girl's innate needs as well, and once again, applied its successful formula during the 1996 Olympics when it selected swimmer Amy Van Dyken and the seven members of the U.S. women's gymnastics team to grace its box. Shannon Miller, from the gymnastics team, commented that it is everyone's dream to be on a Wheaties box. That is a dream shared by all of us, men and women alike, for it represents supremacy on the playing field. Nike, too, taps into a girl's desire to succeed, to master, and to be the best she can be. Their "Just do it" tagline and attitude is as appropriate to girls as it is to boys.

In such a fashion, girls also strive to achieve power as do boys, but they take a different path. In physical form, a girl's power is more apt to be displayed gracefully, such as that achieved in gymnastics as opposed to football. Girls will also play good vanquishing evil as will boys. But whereas a boy will often choose strength to subdue evil, girls will more often first seek the powers of persuasion and nurturing, the aim of which is to change evil into good rather than to subdue it. They are definitely far less aggressive.

Recalls Maya Levinson, a partner at Ogilvy & Mather who spent some fifteen years researching children while at Mattel, "When Mattel introduced She-Ra, Princess of Power dolls for girls, we conducted play-pattern testing. Like most girls, they spent most of the time getting the dolls ready: dressing them, grooming, etc. Finally, one girl had her doll approach the other girl's doll and, speaking through the doll, she asked politely, 'Hi . . . would you like to fight?' in the same exact tone that Ken often asks Barbie out for a date." So Maya was not surprised when, later, her own three-year-old daughter Danielle arranged her brother's Hot Wheels cars in a row, covered them with a cloth diaper, and said, "Shhhh . . . they're sleeping!"

Boys and girls are the same in so many ways, and yet the weight they place on certain values is different. Says John Gray in his book *Men Are from Mars, Women Are from Venus,* "Martians value power, competency, efficiency and achievement. . . . Venusians value love, communication, beauty, and relationships." Kids are no different. Knowing how boys and girls are alike, and how they differ, will help the marketer create and develop successful brands.

Brand Challenges

- Is your brand the best at touching a girl's psyche in one or more ways? Does it or can it help her be or feel
    - beautiful?
    - glamorous?
    - like a mom (nurturing)?
    - silly?
    - like a winner?
    - powerful, in a girl-accepting way?

**N-n-no, we're not scared.
K-keep reading! K-keep reading!**

5

Understand Their Fears

*You gain strength, courage and confidence by every experience
in which you really stop to look fear in the face.*
—Anna Eleanor Roosevelt (1884-1962)

A CHILD'S WORLD IS CONSTANTLY EXPANDING. Cribs turn into
playpens. Playpens vanish and give way to entire homes,
which in turn yield to yards, neighborhoods, cities, and
beyond. With an expanding world comes expanding knowledge of so many things—some good, some not so good.
And as children begin to realize that the amount of control
they possess is minimal, while the world is large and often
beyond their control, they fear.

FEAR: *A distressing emotion aroused by an impending pain,
danger, evil, etc., or by the illusion of such*

Why should a book on children's marketing be concerned with a child's fears? For one, harmless fears can be
entertaining, such as chills a child might feel when watching
the Joker put Batman in peril. It is the peril that makes the
ultimate success so gratifying, to which every filmmaker and
movie-enthusiast will attest. In addition, if you, the marketer,
can actually help resolve a child's fears, thus providing comfort by way of a movie or a toy or a book or whatever, then
you will have found a place in the child's heart. Some
brands have achieved success by soothing a child's fears.

This chapter outlines the many faces of childhood fears. It then explores the implications that such fears yield for marketers. Make no mistake: this chapter is not about exploiting a child's fears, but just the opposite. It is about resolving them and about tickling their fears only in so far that fear delights children—to demonstrate the entertaining peril before the resolution!

The Many Faces of Fear

All children fear something. This is echoed in the book *When Your Child Is Afraid* by Dr. Robert Schachter and Carole Spearin McCauley. Fears are common, as every parent soon discovers, when, from out of nowhere, a child might suddenly state

- "Mom, I don't want you to die."
- "Dad, I'm afraid Danny will beat me up."
- "There's a monster in my closet. I heard him!"

Common fears are also predictable, arising in a natural progression as children grow older and are exposed to a widening set of experiences. Some of these fears are no doubt eternal, particularly those related to survival, while others may reflect the times in which we live. Exhibit #5-1 lists some such fears and the age range within which they commonly arise. It is important, however, to realize that each child is different, so the fears exhibited by any specific child may differ as well. As such, view Exhibit #5-1 in a general sense.

For children about ages five and under whose parents are the critical point of reference, fears are born out of common, parent-related issues. The fears include separation anxiety, manifested in the fear of losing a parent, sometimes brought on by worries about divorce. Other fears include those related to noise, animals, and monsters. As a child's world expands as a result of beginning school, fears take on a new dimension since contact with other children increases dramatically. So, kids begin to fear those

Exhibit #5-1

Fears/Anxieties
And The Age Range Within Which They May Appear
(Partial Listing)

Kids Ages			
0-5	**6-9**	**10-12**	**13-16**
Separation	Social rejection	Kidnapping	Sexual relations
Loss of parent	Criticism	Divorce	Drug use
Divorce	New situations	Personal danger	Crowds
Noises	Burglars	War	Gossip
Animals	Injury	Alone in the dark	Kidnapping
Monsters	Divorce		Terrorism
	Personal danger		Divorce
	War		Personal danger
	Animals		War
	Monsters		

instances that will expose them to the scrutiny of other kids. The range of fears include fear of social rejection, fear of criticism, and the fear of new situations. And since these children are learning more about the world, they begin to fear those things that might threaten them physically, such as injury, burglars, and war.

Kids ages ten to twelve are still dependent on parents, yet they are able to see the greater independence afforded to teens. They are between both worlds and are often referred to as *tweens* (see chapter 9). During this time, they tend to leave childhood fears behind such as those related to monsters and noises, but they have those fears more grounded in real-world issues such as fear of kidnapping, personal danger, or war. Teens find a whole host of new fears that include the fear of sexual relations, drug use, crowds, gossip, and once again, divorce.

Implications for Marketers

A child wishes to experience harmless fears, in small doses, because they are fun. Movies come to mind to illustrate this. Other fears are more personal, involving, and relate to real or perceived threats that no child wants to endure. Divorce and crime might fit this description. These threats are direct assaults on safety and confidence, two needs that children seek to satisfy. Fight or flight are the only two options a child has. And while flight is enticing, it is in mastering and conquering a fear that a child finds the greatest reward, as do we all. Facing the fear makes a child feel more independent, safer, freer, older, more mature, and even brave.

These are all powerful emotional needs, and the marketer who can help comfort a child by resolving a fear will have gained a loyal patron as will that marketer who can entertain a child with gentle fear that results in delight.

Resolving Fears with Things

Marketers have helped resolve fears and comfort a child with *things*. If children are afraid to go asleep by themselves, give them something to hug. If they are afraid of the dark, give them something with light. If they are afraid of intruders, give them a way to chase intruders away. It sounds easy, and it has been for many successful brands.

Stuffed animals have always been a way to ease a child's fears at night. When a child hugs a teddy bear, he is comforted with the presence of a friend. So Playskool markets Gloworm, a friendly, soft worm that glows in the dark when a child hugs it, thus allowing the child to be comforted with both a friend and illumination. Similarly, Huglight Mickey is a soft, huggable Mickey Mouse that has cheeks that glow when the toy is hugged. Its packaging claims, "He's your cuddly companion at bedtime, naptime, anytime!" Another product called the BoogieBuster kit was designed by a mother to help a child defend himself against ghosts and goblins. The kit comes with a storybook, a night-light, and angel tears, which, some say, the boogieman fears.

Mattel introduced My Watch Dog, a cuddly, plush police dog guardian with motion sensors that sensed when someone entered a child's room. Once the intruder was detected, the dog alerted his master with a flashing light and a wailing siren contained in the dog's helmet. The toy also made growling and barking sounds. Children could sleep with ease knowing that no one—and no monsters—could quietly creep up on them as long as My Watch Dog was near.

Brands such as these help ease a child's worries until the day the child no longer needs them. They provide the emotional benefits of safety, comfort, and confidence.

Fears As Entertainment

Storytelling has traditionally used fears as a central part of both conflict and resolution. *Kidnapped*, a masterpiece written by Robert Louis Stevenson in the late 1800s, is one such tale. It is a wonderful piece of literature whose very core touched a timeless fear buried deep within the child: that of being stolen from your home. Specifically, it is the tale of an orphan named David Balfour whose uncle cheats him out of an inheritance and then has him kidnapped and sold into slavery. And while we today may feel far removed from the "circumstances" of the specific dangers Stevenson wrote about (few of us today worry about being sold into slavery by a wicked uncle), the core of this fear, that of being kidnapped, is as real today as ever.

But the hero of this story, and so many others Mr. Stevenson wrote about, faced a fear and resolved it. The boy survived. He beat it. He triumphed over the kidnapping, over a shipwreck, over a hazardous journey across Scotland, and plenty more. And every kid who reads this story from generation to generation imagines that he, too, if put in a similar position, could beat that danger as well. Stories such as these put the fear in a child's face and show that, through bravery, endurance, skill, and intelligence, the fear can be resolved.

The successful movie *Home Alone,* backed by Twentieth Century Fox, touched upon very similar themes in 1990. It is a tale about a boy who is inadvertently left at home by himself, forgotten by his family as they rushed off toward their vacation. While our hero, Kevin, played by Macaulay Culkin, first relishes his newfound independence, a threat soon comes in the form of burglars. But Kevin quickly faces his fears and goes on the offensive, turning his home into a fort. Through smarts, skill, ingenuity, and strength he vanquishes the burglars. It was power, another enduring part of a kid's psyche, that the film touched, and kids around the world felt the rush. For they, too, have fears of being victims of crime. And now they, too, could imagine the same successful outcome. When Kevin beat the bad guys in *Home Alone,* so did children everywhere. Fear resolution is a powerful dimension of fun. John Hughes, who wrote and produced the film, understood that place within a child's psyche that says, "I can take care of myself. I can endure." And such knowledge was profitable, for *Home Alone* was the number-one money-making film in 1990.

Nickelodeon addresses a child's fears with a program entitled "Are You Afraid of the Dark?" The series brings stories of ghosts, goblins, witches, spirits, and the like into a kid's home each week. Each week a different child is confronted with a fearful threat, and each week he triumphs over it—a simple and effective scenario. The fears are eternal, but the situations are updated and made contemporary, just the formula that makes for long-term success.

Characters have been born out of childhood fears. Casper, the friendly yet lonely ghost, was created in the late 1940s by Joe Oriole. It began as a children's book, became a cartoon, then a comic-book figure, a television series, then years later, a movie. Casper is unique. While he is a ghost, he was not a frightful character at all, but a nurturing one.

Now, if the ghosts are evil, who you gonna call? That's right, *Ghostbusters*. The film pitted four rather comic heroes against a great and coming apocalyptic doom. It was the number-one movie at the box office in 1984. The movie was part science, part fantasy, part Halloween—definitely good versus evil. Yet the contrast to Casper is a good one. For the storyteller, ghosts are neither good nor bad, right nor wrong. They are merely props that a creative mind can use as he experiments with different parts of the child's psyche. Casper is nurturing, so you want to love and help him. Other ghosts are not, so you want to destroy them.

Fears are challenging. Facing those fears and beating them are grand for the child. It makes him feel older, more mature, brave. So "Face Your Fears!" taunts the advertising for the Jurassic Park Ride at Universal Studios in Hollywood. Such advertising is a challenge in itself, a tossing down of the gauntlet to see who among us is brave enough to pick it up, to ride the ride, to face our fears. This is all harmless fun. There are no real dinosaurs waiting for us. There are no real raptors, no real T-Rex that will gobble us whole. But, just by challenging us to face our fear, the advertising touches a part of our kid-soul that thinks, "Maybe this time it's real. Maybe this time the ride is too intense. Maybe this time I'll crumble." Then, when we have ridden the ride with our ten-year-olds and have been frightened momentarily by all the special effects, we can all walk out into the parking lot and be able to say to ourselves, "We did it!" Of course, our ten-year-olds will then tell everyone at school that they accomplished what so many others were too chicken to do. For the child, the fun is in the pride and accomplishment generated by the thrills. That is what facing the fear can do. In fact, Universal Studios offers many vicarious experiences that balance against customers' more mundane, everyday lives. "Once they can distinguish between fantasy and reality," says Danny Kaye, vice-president of marketing research at Universal Studios, "children and adults of all ages reach out for entertainment that challenges their senses by thrilling, exciting, unnerving, and even scaring them, for they understand that everything will be all right in the end."

A Fearful Ever-Cool

The book series *Goosebumps* is a good example of the Ever-Cool formula applied to fears of the entertaining variety. Its creator, author R. L. Stine, creates a plethora of contemporary kids, places them in situations that inspire common fears (e.g., being lost, evil magic, monsters, etc.), and then pens their way to a successful resolution. The familiar *Goosebumps* logos can now be found on everything from school binders to partyware to blankets. Dr. Glen Aylward, a child psychologist and professor of psychiatry and pediatrics with the SIU School of Medicine in Springfield, Illinois, told the *State Journal-Register* that "learning to handle a little fright in small stages is a part of growing up." A small fear, faced and overcome, makes way for the real end benefits of pride and accomplishment. That truth must work for R. L. Stine, because the *Goosebumps* book series is reportedly selling at a rate of 5 million books each month with more than 150 million books in print since 1992. The print medium, like programming, is one that allows its successful author to invent contemporary characters and situations, book after book. When there is a substantial number of books in the series, there is enough depth to keep both the current and the next generation of kids interested for years. Thus, you have an Ever-Cool.

Brand Challenges

- Can your brand help resolve a child's fears?
- Or can you create an entertaining story that demonstrates how children have overcome fears of their own?

6

Help Them Gain Control

For only Zeus is free.
—Aeschylus (525-456 B.C.)

THINK BACK TO WHEN YOU WERE A KID. Typically, your mom woke you up in the morning and told you it was time for school. "Hurry," she would repeat more than once during breakfast. "You're late." At school, your teachers told you what to study, when to study it, and then tested you on the material whether you felt prepared or not. School officials told you when to have lunch, when to go to assembly, and when to go home. When you arrived home, your parents told you when to do your homework, when you could play and with whom, when you could have dinner, when you could watch television, what programs you could watch, and finally, when to go to bed so you could start the whole process over again.

CONTROL: *To exercise restraint or direction over*

Simply put, kids have very little control over the world in which they live. Therefore, they love to gain any measure of control over their sphere of existence. Some measures of control that they cherish are grand and fanciful, while others are small and tangible. And we will examine several ways in which obtaining control can be a thrill, indeed. Control touches a strong need that children have to be independent,

71

Dear Santa,
All I want for Christ-
mas is a single remote
that controls the TV,
VCR, sterio, bedtime,
homework and the
dinner
menu.

to make their own choices, to make their own decisions. When they obtain it, kids call it fun.

However, experts call it empowerment. That need for empowerment grows with age, fed each day by every situation that the child cannot control. Brands that provide a child with a measure of control, by making him feel empowered, have the potential to be successful. Some have become Ever-Cools.

Controlling the Uncontrollable

When you control nothing, the greatest desire is to control everything. That is the greatest power of all—to control all things and all situations, to bend them to your will, to tame nature and society all at once. That is a powerful force, indeed.

And so a story about Luke Skywalker was born, a boy whose beginnings sprang from a small, sleepy planet in some corner of some far away galaxy and terribly out of the mainstream of anything worth pursuing until, of course, destiny pits him against an immense evil in the form of Darth Vader. This is the setting, of course, for the *Star Wars* saga, the story of a boy who would eventually master and control the "Force," that mythical energy that, as his teacher Yoda explains, "surrounds us and binds us." With the "Force," Luke gradually learns to move physical objects with the power of his mind alone. He could also bend the wills of others to serve his purpose. And importantly, he could use that power to save a galaxy from the "Dark Side of the Force," that entity that uses the power for evil. Imagine, an entire galaxy depending on one boy coming of age and upon his ability to master and control all things, big and small. The movie had all the elements: good versus evil, power, great risk, control and mastery, and the eventual confidence to succeed. "I don't believe it!" said an inexperienced Luke as he saw Yoda levitate his ship. "That is why you fail," Yoda retorts. And finally in the third film of the trilogy,

Return of the Jedi, we see the knight we knew that Luke would become: brave, fearless, in control, powerful, and good.

Every child, large and small, who saw the *Star Wars* trilogy could imagine that they, too, might find that illusive power that would allow mere mortals to gain control over the uncontrollable. Make no mistake, this is a powerful emo-tion that finds it way into fantasy, and the marketer who can touch this part of a kid's psyche can make it big. Clearly, George Lucas, who wrote and directed *Star Wars,* under-stands the soul of the child, that child within all of us. And yet it took years of effort until he found a studio, Twentieth Century Fox, to give a green light to the *Star Wars* project. The studio sank only ten million dollars into a film that would launch the greatest movie-making saga of all time.

But George Lucas and the executives at Twentieth Century Fox were clever marketers as well. They turned *Star Wars* into an Ever-Cool by using some smart marketing strategies. First, and fortuitously, evil was not destroyed after the first film. So when it did well at the box office, evil lin-gered on through *The Empire Strikes Back* and *Return of the Jedi* until its demise. Importantly, these were not "constructed" as stand-alone films, but as *episodes* in a much larger story. And instead of numbering these first three films as I, II, and III, they were numbered IV, V, and VI. This, in fact, means that *Star Wars* fans have to wait for the day when George Lucas decides to enlighten us on the happenings in the ear-lier years of the galaxy with episode films I, II, and III, which are now in the works. In this way, the *Star Wars* saga not only touched its audience's psyche, it was structured in a way to re-invent itself with highly anticipated, future films. This marketing strategy was brilliant in its simplicity and execut-ed marvelously with a fast-paced, engaging story bathed in wondrous special effects. Hence, Lucas discovered a way to target the childlike emotions in all of us while perpetuating the *Star Wars* phenomenon. This is one of the best applica-tions of the Ever-Cool formula ever devised.

Superman, of course, is the contemporary icon from which many such recent characters sprang. In Superman, we have a superhero whose powers are far above those of mortal men and women and who uses them for good in order to bring peace and decency to a world that is out of control. Superman is about power, control, and bringing right to where there was only wrong. The character comes back into the forefront now and again, brought to life by movies, television programs, and comic books.

In H. G. Wells' *The Time Machine,* the hero controlled time. Dr. Frankenstein controlled life itself and brought his creature back from the dead. In the continuing *Star Trek* saga, the very popular character of Q controls both time and space. In Greek mythology, the gods controlled many aspects of nature.

As referenced earlier, Nickelodeon's successful series, "The Secret World of Alex Mack," touches on control as well, this time starring a girl who accidentally obtains supernatural powers that allow her to thwart neighborhood evils. She can control her own physical form, as well as other physical objects. The 1996 release of the film *Matilda,* based upon a book by Roald Dahl, introduces us to a girl who discovers she can use her mind to control her environment, very similar to Alex Mack, Luke Skywalker, and so many other stories that touch a child's need to feel empowered.

Controlling Others

Not many kids can actually control the uncontrollable. So their best bet is to control those around them, if they can. "Control" in this sense is nothing more than wielding some degree of influence. It is not manipulation. It is simply feeling empowered. And as fate would have it, there is one group of individuals that a kid would most love to have some influence over—parents.

Man-o-man, how fun it would be to gain some influence over your parents. Every time a girl asks her parents to stop at McDonald's instead of somewhere else, and they do it, she wields a bit of influence. It makes her feel important, as though she had an opinion, and someone in authority listened, appreciated, and acted. In fact, every parent knows that giving a child a choice of tasks always produces better results than if you give a child no choice. So, if you ask Billy to do his homework, you are apt to get more complaining than if you ask Billy to do his homework, then allow him to choose whether he does it before or after dinner. Given a choice, Billy is more likely to choose the one that fits him best and he will feel good that he had at least some control and input into the decision.

Control over parents can manifest itself in a few concrete ways. Children everywhere cheer when Bart Simpson outwits his dad, Homer. That is a very appealing part of the storyline. For the 1984 advertising of the male action line of He-Man, a commercial depicted a boy playing with his He-Man figure, who vanquished the evil Skeletor figure in the hands of the boy's dad. Kids loved the power. They loved to save a universe, and they loved it when the boy played with his dad and won. For just a moment, across the nation, boys everywhere gained just a bit of control.

Controlling Things

Children love to master the world about them. That mastery provides increments and milestones toward their maturity. Controlling everyday objects can provide such a feeling. This comes in several forms.

Controlling Personal Choice

We have already alluded to the importance of allowing children to choose between alternatives. This not only empowers them, but it also provides an outlet for personal choice and expression. Jane may like plain potato chips, but Irene likes barbecue-flavored ones. Paul might prefer rocky road ice cream, but Michelle loves strawberry. Each personal preference makes a child unique. That is important.

Paint 'N Dazzle Barbie dolls allowed girls to color and deco-rate Barbie's clothes. The dolls came with fabric paint and vari-ous decorations such as glitter, rosettes, and rhinestones. Each girl could express her own sense of beauty and creativity. This individual expression allows each outcome to be different, each tailored to the artistic impression of the individual girl. This product allows control, expression, and individuality.

Barbie Fashion Designer, a software product introduced by Mattel in 1996, allows a girl to design a Barbie fashion on her computer screen. In this way, the girl has direct control of a Barbie doll's fashion—the style, the color, the look. With the touch of a button, she can print the design on fabric that fits a standard computer's printer. Then she can dress her Barbie doll up in her own fashion creation. Now that is control, not one born of strength and power, but one born of glamour, combined with an ounce of individuality. This product may become an Ever-Cool if appealing software is introduced year after year to keep the fashions and play themes current.

Showbiz Pizza Time prides itself on developing the Chuck E. Cheese's concept in a way that empowers chil-dren. "Whereas family restaurants will only have a kid's menu and a few crayons," says Dick Huston, executive vice-president for Showbiz Pizza Time, "Chuck E. Cheese's offers a full kid-experience where they feel empowered to make many choices on their own—which games to play, which rides to ride, and which toys to choose when they redeem the tickets they've won." In effect, with the tokens, games, and winnings, Chuck E. Cheese's allows the child to have control. Also, Chuck E. Cheese's is kept contemporary with remodeling and added experiences that continue to appeal to a child's emotional needs.

Controlling Objects

The previous element of control dealt with choice, which is really an issue of control over preference and individuali-ty. Here we discuss manual control, and kids love it.

Few adults can forget when remote-controlled cars were first brought to market. They were a huge success because they allowed children to control something that was far removed from themselves. Electric race cars provided a similar thrill. The hairpin turns, the straight-away, the loop are all a test of the child's ability to control the play.

Control can come in whimsical forms. For example, we are all familiar with the PEZ Candy dispenser referenced in chapter 2. Just pull back Bugs Bunny's head and out pops a tasty candy treat. Sure, the candy could have been in a plain plastic wrapper, but it is the dispenser, both its licensed characters and the control it provides, that makes it fun. A bit of control turns candy into a plaything, a thing to take places, a thing to be seen with. And every so often, PEZ Candy changes the characters in order to keep the dispenser current with the times. Again, here we have the Ever-Cool formula applied.

There are, of course, other examples of products that provide children with control. There is the Push-Up, a sherbet treat that is pushed up through a cardboard tube with a stick. The ability to "control" the ice cream is one dimension of its fun. A Spin Pop candy has a battery-operated holder that, at the push of a button, spins a lollipop in a circle. The kid just pops the lollipop in her mouth, pushes the button, and the spin is automatic—no more twirling of the fingers to get the same affect. Screw Ups is a small, clear plastic, motorized candy dispenser that takes small beaded candies and pushes them up a conveyor belt to an opening. Dannon's Sprinkl'ins yogurt allows kids to add sprinkles to their yogurt. In a category of "do-nothing" yogurts, this brand suddenly empowered a child with a small measure of control, and it was a success.

An Empowering Ever-Cool

I lived through the dark days of the videogame category in the early 1980s, when huge brands like Intellivision and

Atari went from boom to bust in a matter of months, when the quality of the software evaporated, when demand vanished. Yet out of the ashes came another player, one with the quality and the excitement to relaunch the entire category. Its name was Nintendo. With a little plumber named Mario, it set the market on fire. And marketers and analysts everywhere deem these game *fun*. But just what type of fun is this?

Nintendo offers many types of fun. There is good vanquishing evil. The player faces the challenge of surviving one level and advancing to the next. With each success he experiences pride in his accomplishment. And the sound and graphics that brought the game to life add to its realism. And Nintendo adds one more ingredient: empowerment born from control. The child can *live* through the characters by taking on their lives, their situations, and controlling their actions. When a child *enters* the game, he is in a world made by others, but he gradually gains control as his skill and mastery evolve. Says George Harrison, vicepresident of marketing at Nintendo, "Kids realize that the real world is a big place. Nintendo allows them to control a world of their own, to control their own destiny. Nintendo 64 [newest system launched in 1996] then rewards them at the end of each level, acknowledging their accomplishment so they can feel good about themselves." In fact, the very idea that a small, nonthreatening character like Mario can succeed is important, noted Mr. Harrision, because it means you do not have to be like Arnold Schwarzenegger to survive.

Nintendo stays contemporary in several ways. First, a flow of new, more sophisticated systems every few years keeps the Nintendo brand current and cool. They provide more engaging graphics, quality, and control. Also, "Good story-telling is timeless," says Mr. Harrison, so the importance of getting the story right is key. Finally, the software library pushes Nintendo onward year after year, for in the end, the game is the thing.

"If you add up the box-office grosses of the top 11 films of all time," says Mr. Harrision, "the worldwide receipts total about $3.2 billion, whereas the total worldwide retail sales of the 11 Mario games is about $6.4 billion . . . testimony to the place Mario has won in the hearts and minds of kids." Nintendo has mastered the Ever-Cool formula.

Brand Challenges

- Can your brand help a child be or feel more in control?
- Can it empower him with a story, or with control over choice or over physical things?
- Can you develop a new brand in a normally "do-nothing" product category and insert an ounce of control for the child to wield and to cherish?

7

Embrace Their Fantasies

*The dream is the small hidden door in the deepest
and most intimate sanctum of the soul.*
—Carl Gustav Jung (1875-1961)

THERE ARE MILLIONS OF CHILDREN who are driven by core emotions related to their innate gender, to a growing list of fears that spring from greater contact with an immense world, and to their desire to control a world that they cannot.

But when a child realizes he cannot control the things around him, his only recourse is to fantasize that he can. Yes, adults do the same, but for children, the fantasy is greater because the lack of control is greater. Hence, fantasy becomes an everyday part of a child's life, woven throughout the waking day. A parent will tell a child for the nth time, for example, to do his homework and then finds him just minutes later sitting motionless over his schoolwork. The books are open and scattered about, but his gaze is directed out the window, his eyes fixed on something beyond the physical world—to a place where there is no homework or household rules or that spelling test on Friday. It is a place where physical laws of nature do not apply, where desire and fulfillment meet—in a daydream.

Then a parent ruins the moment with a hearty scolding, "Johnny! How many times must I tell you to do your

homework. If you would just bear down and get it done, you would have completed it by now." But the dream, so enticing and fulfilling, keeps coming back in a thousand different ways. It is hard to suppress, particularly if it is a daydream that relates to prominent fantasies, because it goes down deep to the core of desire, to the child's very heart, to the wishes that whisper constantly for that which he yearns—control, achievement, pride, recognition, love, and acceptance.

FANTASY: *Imagination, especially when extravagant and unrestrained*

Marketers who understand and embrace a child's fantasies will survive the ages. They know that daydreams are not just fanciful moments of whimsy; they are windows to the soul. Exhibit #7-1 reveals some of the most prominent top-of-mind childhood fantasies obtained by asking children "If you could have two wishes come true, what would they be?" The answers are abundant. Among other things, children want to be rich, to be empowered by being older or stronger, to be famous either in professional sports or in a career. While girls' and boys' fantasies differ in expected ways, in others they are similar, particularly when it comes to riches and empowerment. Other fantasies are simple manifestations of other, more encompassing ones. This is the case of a child's wish to drive. Such a wish is, in reality, one concrete expression of the child's desire to be older and more empowered. Still other fantasies may be a reflection of our times, such as solving world problems or resolving problems within the family.

"Brands that are successful," says Irma Zandl, trend expert and president of The Zandl Group, "tend to have a superior understanding of kids' emotional needs as well as the creative firepower to tap their fantasies and dreams." This is so true. What follows is a review of some of the most prominent of these fantasy themes and how some astute

Exhibit #7-1

Kids' Wish List

	8-12 year olds	
	Boys	**Girls**
Be Rich	57%	53%
Sports (e.g., Go pro)	23%	–
Empowerment (e.g., Be older/stronger/fly)	18%	12%
Wheels (e.g., Drive)	16%	7%
Entertainment (e.g., Videogames)	10%	–
Career/Success (e.g., Fame)	9%	8%
Meet a Celebrity	–	10%
Romance	9%	9%
Family (e.g., Health/togetherness)	–	15%
Solve world problems	6%	12%
School (e.g., Be smart)	4%	–
Appearance	–	6%
Pets	3%	10%
Travel	3%	8%

Source: 1995 Zandl Report, The Zandl Group

marketers have fulfilled them. And in fulfilling these fantasies, the marketers have either created new brands, contemporized existing ones, or created enticing stories and characters for use in films, books, and elsewhere that captured a child's heart. One brand among them has become a massive, fantasy Ever-Cool.

"I Wish I Were Rich"

The story of *Cinderella* is the most prominent of rags-to-riches tales, taking our heroine from a life of tattered clothes, no romance, and an abusive step-family to one with a fairy godmother, a glass slipper, and a prince. This story is an ancient one, and its longevity is testimony to its powerful ability to touch a child's heart. *Cinderella* fulfills the desire for freedom, independence, control, and justice.

The comic-book character of Richie Rich was born of this fantasy as well. Money bought him the big house, the fast car, the planes, the boats—everything. It was a fantasy kids could relate to and cherish; they responded by reading the comic books published by Harvey Famous Comics, watching the cartoon based upon the character in the 1980s, and, finally, buying theater tickets for the movie in the 1990s that grossed more than eighty million dollars.

Promotions can make a child feel rich. A recent Post Pebbles cereal commercial depicted Fred and Barney, of "The Flintstones" fame, finding treasure in a pyramid. "Now that we've found the treasure, you can win $1,000 in gold coins," declared Fred. And that is not all: the sweepstakes winners also received a year's supply of the cereal. This sweepstakes ties right into a child's fantasy to be rich, both in gold and in product. Such programs help keep brands contemporary.

Now, if you can get rich by controlling expensive property, that could be a tasty fantasy, indeed. That is the very essence of the MONOPOLY board game. This game affords each player the opportunity to be a powerful land baron or a landless jail bird, all in an afternoon. It has it all: fortune building, competition, and chance. The MONOPOLY game so astutely fulfills a kid's "get rich" fantasy that no other game has come close to bumping it off. Since 1935, more than 160 million copies of the game have been sold, and more than 480 million people, across 75 countries and 26 languages, have played it. It seems that a well-developed game can become an Ever-Cool without much contemporizing other than cosmetic changes. Good games have "built-in" appeal that keeps a player coming back. Each time he plays, he has a different experience. He finds himself in different situations, perhaps with different opponents. And the more he plays, the better strategist he becomes. Hence, mastery, chance, the potential fulfillment of a key fantasy, and the thrill of winning and the risk of losing can all blend to make an Ever-Cool.

"I Wish I Were Big"

That empowering phrase has been uttered by countless children over the ages and finally found its way into the script of the movie *Big*, in which a twelve-year-old boy makes a wish to be big and then watches it come true the next morning as he wakes and discovers that he is older and bigger and, well, the actor Tom Hanks. Of course, the child finds that it is not so great to be big, for there are a lot of responsibilities that come with the added years. But at the time that he wished to be big, the twelve-year-old could only see the dream. That dream to be big is nothing less than a dream for freedom and control.

Typically, children want to be a few years older than whatever age they are at a given moment. Why? Because a child can readily see and appreciate the freedom and control afforded the slightly older child. The five-year-old sees that his older brother can stay up later. The ten-year-old girl stays home while seeing her older sister excitedly dash out to her first date. The seven-year-old boy sees the eleven-year-old boys on the playground who "rule" and he can't wait for the day when he, too, is one of the big kids on the playground.

Big also allows the child to fantasize about obtaining a greater degree of his gender-specific desires. For boys, being older gets you bigger muscles, faster feet, and the girl of your dreams. For girls, being older gets you a more mature figure, a bigger circle of friends, and the boy of your dreams. Both sexes wish for that car to zip around in.

If a child cannot really become big, then perhaps he can

be made to feel big. Children's cosmetics make the seven-year-old girl feel older. A ten-speed bike makes the nine-year-old feel like a teen, even though his legs cannot stretch comfortably to the pedals yet.

Some marketers have successfully demonstrated how their brands can help the child achieve getting bigger. A past advertising campaign for the National Dairy Board is one example. One commercial within the campaign showed an older boy of, say fifteen or so, standing next to a younger girl of about twelve. He ignores her completely, looking in the other direction. The girl, undaunted by the rebuke, begins to drink her milk, and as she does, we see her grow older, maturing, until she is about twenty and quite attractive. Yet she is still standing next to the boy who now looks rather small and childish in comparison. All the time she is growing, we hear her talk about the virtues of milk: that it will give her a lot of what she needs for strong bones, beautiful skin, and a great smile. This will help her "outside" catch up to the beautiful person she is on the "inside." And when she is fully mature, she declares to the boy that she will have "long since outgrown you, and you'll be history." The campaign says, "Milk. It does a body good." This campaign connected the product's attributes to real fantasies desired by children and made the campaign nothing less than a mirror reflecting the dream that lives within the heart of a child. The benefits were not merely rational (e.g., strong bones and beautiful skin) but also emotional (e.g., confidence and empowerment).

"I Wish I Were Famous"

Fame is empowering, and some brands attempt to attach themselves to the "fame" fantasy in hopes it will connect them with kids. McDonald's, for example, ran an advertising campaign with the theme "If kids ran the world." In one spot, a boy dreams of fame, specifically, of playing basketball in the NBA. "I'd be in the NBA," he says. "I'd have my own agent." In fact, he declares, "Everyone would want my autograph." As he is speaking, we see the fantasy unfold around him. And after the big game, his fantasy takes him to McDonald's, of course. The brand, in essence, hitched a ride on a kid's fantasy in order to create a deeper relationship between the child and the brand.

Most boys have these sports-related daydreams. Most men do as well. The sports fantasy has its roots in a boy's desire for power through strength and speed. To make the game-winning point with only a second left on the clock is the sweetest. Girls will fantasize about fame as well, and it might take any number of forms including being a singer, dancer, actress, or world-class gymnast. There is a grace in this fame, and it finds its mark in the girl's desire for glamour and agility.

Brands have taken other routes as well to hitch a ride on the fame bus. The largest promotion in the history of Oscar Mayer entailed a talent search in ninety cities across America. The children auditioned by singing either the "Wiener Jingle" or the "Bologna Song," long associated with the brand. Winners were chosen to be in an Oscar Mayer television commercial. That is *real* fame! Heinz USA introduced the Heinz Ketchup Creative Design Awards, which invited kids to design a new label for the brand. The winning entries were to be reproduced on a limited edition of the bottles. These examples not only provide a chance of fame for the child, but they also appeal to the parent who already believes that his child is a star.

In another example, the San Diego Padres shattered the imaginary line that exists between their famous players and their kid fans. They began a program that allowed kids to be part of the baseball experience, part of the fame. They invited kids onto the field to meet the players, to talk to them, to touch them, to run the bases, to interact in various ways with the game itself. In doing so, they have allowed kids to be close to the spotlight, to taste the fame. Such experiences breed loyalty.

"I Wish My Home/Family/World Were . . . "

As times change, so too do some fantasies. As the divorce rate soared, more kids wished that their families would stay together. As friends move away due to a parent's job displacement, kids seek greater, more solid friendships. As children are exposed to reports of crime either through television or firsthand experience, they dream of being safe in their beds at night. As they hear about wars in faraway places, they fantasize about a world filled with peace and dream that their neighborhood will be protected. These create powerful fantasies that demand fulfillment, and many marketers have met that challenge in unique ways. This will be described in chapters 11 and 12, which detail how marketers have fulfilled needs created by both a child's greater awareness of the world and a shifting family structure.

The list of fantasies is also as vast as the number of children, each of whom finds himself in a different circumstance that demands a different dream. If a child thinks he is not as smart as others, he will want to become smarter. If a child believes she is less attractive than others, she will want to be more attractive. If he perceives himself to be weak, he will want strength. If she cannot fly, she will want wings.

THE TRANSFORMATION: *To change in form, appearance, or structure; metamorphose*

Fantasies cannot come true, in reality or pretend, unless we add a critical ingredient. That ingredient is the belief in transformation. This is the catalyst component of the fantasy, the part that makes the fantasy happen. When the child daydreams, he may be fantasizing about winning a race with a boy he never beat before or playing an instrument flawlessly. In each case, the child transformed himself in a way that would allow the wish to be fulfilled. He was not the fastest runner. Now he is. He could not play the violin well. Now he can.

As noted earlier by the milk campaign example, some marketers have demonstrated this transformation in advertising. When done well, the depiction of the transformation can be powerful. Another example was the introductory commercial for Nerf Bow and Arrow. In the spot, a boy is running through a forest with the Nerf Bow and Arrow in hand, supposed dangers all around. The boy then jumps onto a log and jets into the air. We see him as he flies across the screen. As he does, he suddenly transforms into a full-grown, Rambolike character before landing on the ground once again. But now he is big and strong, muscles bulging, with a confident gaze in his all-knowing eyes. He still grips the Nerf Bow and Arrow as he continues his battle to thwart evil. I once showed this commercial in focus groups some years along, buried in a reel of many others. I asked the eight-year-old boys sitting around me to applaud when they saw a scene in any of the commercials that they particularly liked. I pushed the button and let all the commercials run. When that scene appeared, where the boy transformed into a fully grown Rambolike character, the boys jumped to their feet and applauded and cheered. The commercial, in essence, was a mirror, and the boys saw their fantasy reflected back in the context of the brand.

The Storyteller's Toolbox

Transformation is also a powerful storytelling device, and there are four storytelling paths that a child's fantasy can take, via transformation, for a wish to be fulfilled—by way of achievement, magic, science, or dumb luck. When fantasies and transformational paths collide, what results are many story directions for kid-directed movies, television programs, or children's books. The movie *The Mighty Ducks* was about a hapless kids' ice-hockey team that, through raw teamwork and *achievement,* won the championship no one thought was possible. *Cinderella* went from rags to riches via *magic.* The boy hero of the movie *Weird Science* obtained his heart's desire via *science,* by using his home computer to create a superbeing, in the form of a supermodel.

Let us say, as an example, that a child is struggling in school and wishes to get better grades. There are four ways the fantasy can be resolved:

- *Achievement:* The child bears down, studies hard, and makes the grade. This sounds like an afterschool special or perhaps an episode of Nickelodeon's cartoon "Doug," the series about a good-hearted boy who faces everyday hurdles and always resolves them while he learns much in the process.

- *Magic:* The child, instead, could find a shiny, magical stone that was inadvertently dropped by a passing wizard. The boy makes a wish and—zap!—instant smarts. It sounds like a storybook.

- *Science:* Perhaps our hero, instead, decides to hook his computer to his headphones, and he then turns on the juice. Zap! A billion bits of data shoot into the boy's brain, thus producing instant smarts. It sounds like a 1970 film called *The Computer Wore Tennis Shoes.*

- *Dumb luck:* Perhaps the child is taking some true/false IQ test and decides to answer every even question with a true and every odd question with a false. By happenstance, he gets 100 percent. Everybody thinks he is a genius, which sets up humorous situations and a moral dilemma for our young lad. It sounds like an episode of "Family Matters."

In each case, we would add a moral to be learned or a responsibility to be accepted and resolved. But it all begins with the fantasy and the paths of achievement, magic, science, and luck that are the playthings for creative minds. I have used them in many brainstorming sessions for people in a variety of fields, from film to animation to advertising. They can be powerful tools for creating stories in themselves or creating stories that envelop brands. There is more on this subject in chapter 16.

The Reigning Fantasy Ever-Cool

One Ever-Cool stands alone in its ability to own fantasy and the magic often associated with making dreams come true. This brand, of course, is Disney.

Cinderella, Snow White and the Seven Dwarfs, Beauty and the Beast, Toy Story—each is based upon a fantasy, a transformation, an engaging tale that touches our hearts. Each year Disney introduces children to new characters through which children can experience heartaches, fears, challenges, and triumph—all dipped in magic. While Disney cannot claim to be the originator of each story it tells (*Cinderella,* for example, is an ancient fairy tale that originated in the Orient and developed into some 500 variations existing in European folklore), Disney knows how to bring stories to life in such a grand and fanciful way that Disney is forever associated with them. Disneyland, itself, is the place where such stories and fantasies come alive before a child's eyes, where he can meet a character of his dreams one moment, and be hurled through space or slide down the Matterhorn the next. Says the plaque over the entrance of Disneyland, "Here You Leave Today And Enter The World Of Yesterday, Tomorrow And Fantasy."

Disney seems to understand one more critical factor. When you satisfy a child's hopes, dreams, and fantasies, you have the potential to capture the child that still lives within each of us. Witness the success of *The Little Mermaid, Aladdin, The Lion King,* and other movies. Baby boomers everywhere saw those films and relived a part of their own youth. For just a brief moment, in darkened theaters, clutching a bag of buttered popcorn, sitting next to our own kids, we were young again, and again, and again.

No other brand has come close to achieving what Disney has in this arena. It is pure fantasy, an Ever-Cool brand that has a deep relationship with kids, young and old, because it understands the dreams that exist within their hearts. It is interesting to note that in the early 1930s, a New York businessman offered Walt Disney $300 for the right to put the image of Mickey Mouse on stationery. In 1996, Disney revenues topped $18 billion.

Brand Challenges

- Is your brand embracing a child's fantasies? Could it? Should it?
- Does your brand help a child be or feel
    - richer?
    - bigger or older?
    - famous?
    - better connected to family, friends, and the world?
- Can you craft a story that brings any of another million fantasies to life via achievement, magic, science, or luck?
- Can you touch the child's heart in all of us?

No, ma'am, he isn't hurt. On the contrary, he just set
the school record for the most atomic
turbo fireballs eaten at one time.

8

Gratify Their Senses

*The moment the little boy is concerned with which is a jay
and which is a sparrow, he can no longer
see the birds or hear them sing.*
—Eric Berne (1910-1970)

ADULTS FORGET THE WONDER of a first experience—the first
sound of a child's laughter; the first sight of a scarlet sunset;
the first sweet, intoxicating smell of chocolate. Repeated
experience with such things makes them common to our
perceptions. So, after a time, we pay little attention to the
cheerful sound of children's voices that emanate from a
neighborhood playground. We drive past those sunsets with
only a momentary glance. We stuff the chocolate in our
mouth and swallow it down, not even allowing its smell to
be fully unleashed.

GRATIFY: *To please or satisfy*

But on occasion, every now and again, our adult senses
grab us in unexpected, startling ways. They come alive, but
only because they are stimulated in ways we did not expect.
One such occasion happened to me a few years ago on
Father's Day. My kids rushed into my bedroom at dawn.
They jumped onto my chest and cheerfully thrust a Father's
Day card into my hand. As I rose from a dead sleep to open
it, my wife sat smiling at my side. My eyesight was still

blurred, my ears were prepared for nothing but silence as I read. I opened the card and was stunned by a sudden rush of voices emanating from the card itself. The voices were of my two children wishing me a happy Father's Day. The sound came from a miniature recorder constructed into the card that my children used the day before to record their greeting.

I sat there in disbelief that the card could speak with the voices of my sweet children. My senses were stimulated in a way I did not expect. It was magic. For a brief moment, I felt the wonder that a child feels daily. It was part amusement, part awe, part happiness, part discovery. The sound was so unexpected, it penetrated my senses and drove straight into my brain, then deep into my soul. I was suddenly happy—thrilled, really. I hugged my children and laughed out loud at the experience. If only, I thought, I could feel such amusement all the time. What fun that would be!

And what success a marketer could have if only she could tickle a child's senses in an unexpected way. It could become the genesis of a brand idea or a way to breathe fresh life into an existing one. It could be the start of a brand relationship that lingers on. This is echoed in a comment by Michael Vaughn, executive group director at Ogilvy & Mather New York, responsible for the Hershey brand. "We have extensive evidence that people form their candy-eating preferences and habits very early in life. You constantly hear adults say, 'That brand is one of my favorites. I loved them as a kid.'"

Tickling the senses is one possible starting point for beginning that brand relationship.

Hearing and Sound

There are brands we grew up with that were magic because they captivated our sense of hearing in a way that others did not. Some became mega-brands. When you hear the brand name Kellogg's Rice Krispies cereal, what sound springs to mind? That's right, "Snap! Crackle! Pop!"

Can you think of any other cereal brand that is so uniquely identified with a sound, as well as with a song that brings the sound to life? I cannot. So in developing a unique difference in an otherwise soundless category, the Kellogg Company and its advertising agency crafted a brand that has survived since 1928. And yet it seems so simple; just add sound to a category where there is none, and success just might be yours. This attribute, and the characters that embellish it, has also leapt across borders, although in Sweden it is "Piff! Paff! Puff!" In Germany, "Knisper! Knasper! Knusper!" In Mexico, "Pim! Pum! Pam!" The brand is made contemporary year after year through promotions and advertising and such, but the core of its very existence has more to do with a toasted, puffed rice cereal that makes a noise in milk. We see the humble beginnings of a brand relationship.

Enter Oscar Mayer. With the Wienermobile and Wiener Whistle, Oscar Mayer associated its brand of meats with the movement of a fanciful vehicle and the blow of a whistle. Such miniature whistles have been used as premiums for decades. I had mine in earlier years, as did every kid on my street. And it all sprang from the seemingly odd association of adding a "sound" quality to a hot dog.

General Foods patented the basic idea behind the successful Pop Rocks candy in the 1960s and finally introduced the candy into the United States in 1976. It became an instant hit. In the world of candy treats, there was nothing like it. Just toss a few Pop Rocks candies in your mouth and they crackle and fizz! The invention was a chance event. General Foods was actually looking for a way to make fizzy drinks. In the process, they discovered the innovative idea of encapsulating carbon dioxide in sweets. In the early days of Pop Rocks candies, General Foods was very concerned about oversaturating the market, so they would introduce a candy treat for only a few months and then withdraw it from the market and replace it with another treat, each based on the same crackle and fizz concept. This would prevent the novelty appeal of the treat from wearing off. Hence, they kept the craze going by not oversupplying it, and then they continuously re-invented it. They demonstrate yet another intriguing way to apply the Ever-Cool formula.

Sight

Many marketers incorporate visual treatments around their products in order to gain a child's attention. Videogame manufacturers compete on graphics. The more realistic, as well as the more surrealistic, the better. This is also true for computer games, for comic books, for programming. Among other products: Procter & Gamble introduced a line extension for Crest toothpaste, one with sparkles to appeal to kids. The product's point of difference is its sparkly appearance.

The most intriguing examples arise when a marketer introduces a new dimension of sight into a category that has little to offer. Lazer Pop Candy, a product from Cap Toys, is a long candy stick that has a small light bulb incorporated into its plastic base. Push the button on the base, and the light shines up through the translucent candy pop, highlighting the many colors of the pop itself.

Also, one baker, reported *Supermarket News*, produced bread that came in both rainbow and school colors. Said Dr. Ron Wirtz, director of information services for American Institute of Baking in Manhattan, Kansas, "Anything novel in the bread line can attract their [children's] attention." And apparently adding unique, unexpected colors to bread is a case in point as he went on to tell *Supermarket News*, "They just can't make enough of it."

L.A. Gear introduced L.A. Lights athletic shoes that have small, motion-sensitive flashing lights embedded in their soles. Basically, they blink when you walk. This unique combination of footwear and lights was a success. L.A. Lights shoes took the nation by storm and were the top-selling kids' shoes nationwide in 1993, according to one source. However, sales began to drop dramatically in subsequent years due to the novelty wearing off. The added feature, although engaging, needs to be refreshed year after year. L.A. Gear has yet to figure out how to continuously contemporize the L.A. Lights offering in order to sustain sales at their initial levels.

When it comes to maintaining visual excitement, the Ever-Cool award goes to Crayola crayons. The first box of Crayola crayons was produced in 1903 by Binney & Smith Company, contained 8 colors, and sold for five cents. By the 1950s there were 48 colors. Then came some 72 colors in the 1970s and 1980s, which also witnessed the introduction of fluorescent colors with such names as Laser Lemon, Screamin' Green, and Atomic Tangerine. The 1990s have seen some 96 colors. Crayola crayons touches a child's eternal need to create, to achieve, to feel the pride of accomplishment. They have stayed contemporary with the introduction of interesting colors and themes and even glitter and scented crayons. The Crayola brand has also expanded into many activity arenas. With the Crayola Bubble Painter, a child can create a bubble with paint, then pop it against paper for interesting, "one-of-a-kind designs." With creations like this, the Crayola brand essence is extended across categories while maintaining its contemporary feel.

Smell

Among kid marketers, those who work in the toy business are usually way ahead of the rest in terms of experimenting with new combinations of kid-pleasing product features. That is because toy manufacturers have to reinvent their toy lines every year. Kids do not want last year's toys. They want something new, different, and cool. As a result, toy manufacturers are always experimenting to find a new idea or a fresh way to make an old idea feel new. One approach has been to add fragrance to toys.

So the Strawberry Shortcake doll, introduced in 1980, reigned supreme. The doll smelled like strawberries. Girls flocked to stores everywhere to pick her up, smell her fragrance, and play with her endlessly. It was a refreshing, well-executed approach to an old doll category.

Of course, smells can add a bizarre twist, especially if designed for boys. Nickelodeon's Smell My Gak comes in many fragrances like pizza and popcorn, strange smells for an oozing lump of goo. The children's section of the L.A. City Zoo has a machine that produces various smells at the touch of a button, and a child who pushes the button then attempts to identify the source of the various smells. It is a guessing game, and kids like it.

I cannot think of a current Ever-Cool whose key point of difference revolves around a smell. This is either because of my inability to discover it, or it is an opportunity that remains unfulfilled.

Touch

Place your finger in a newborn baby's palm, and her fingers will close to clutch yours. Yes, it is a reflex, but it demonstrates the importance of this sense to a growing child.

In the world of tactile gratification, we need to pay homage to the first finger-squeeze mega-brand, and that is Play-Doh modeling compound. For approximately forty years, children have poked it, squished it, and stomped on it. Their fingers molded whatever their hearts desired, which shifted over the years as a child's interest changed. To help stay competitive in today's climate, Playskool produced a line of products that extend the brand's play. In 1995 they introduced Play-Doh Jewels and Gems Bracelet Maker to appeal to the girls' psyche and Play-Doh Mad

Monster Creator to appeal to the boys' psyche. In effect, the Play-Doh brand now fulfills many dimensions of a kid's heart. This approach helps keep it contemporary, while it deepens the brand's relationship with its consumers.

Food products can also benefit from this touch and feel appeal. "Kids eat candy to satisfy many different needs," says Kirk Ward, director of consumer and trade research at Hershey Chocolate. "For nonchocolate candy, one of those needs is relief from boredom, or something just to pass the time with. For these occasions, the 'play value' of the candy is critical." So Hershey Chocolate introduced Twizzlers Pull-n-Peel candy, which is a shoestring, licorice-like candy in a thick bundle. Kids peel one strand at a time, play with it, then eat it. "Both the introductory and follow-up advertising campaigns focused on the fun of the product," said Mr. Ward. "The initial campaign gave kids ideas about the different shapes they could make with each Pull-n-Peel strand. Subsequent advertising animated those strands to allow them to 'play' with each other." Hence, Hershey Chocolate invented a candy that not only provided taste appeal, but it also added play value via touch (i.e., pull and peel), shapes (i.e., designs), and even creativity (i.e., pride). At last report, the brand was off to a good start.

In terms of providing *unique* touches, a prize must also go to Kraft General Foods for the Jell-O Jigglers gelatin recipe promotion. The Jigglers recipe is a more concentrated form of Jell-O gelatin that gives it just the density needed to cut it into fanciful shapes and then to hold them in your hand. This is a great appeal to children who have always liked to poke Jell-O gelatin. One way Jigglers stays current is by offering contemporary, special molds with changing, promotional themes: Christmas, Easter, Jurassic Park, alphabet letters, etc. In effect, Kraft General Foods turned Jell-O gelatin into a playful, touchable, finger food, and in so doing, increased sales by 7 percent after the first year of introduction, according to one source. And it all started with a simple commercial featuring Bill Cosby, who declared with excitement, "Now we can eat Jell-O gelatin with our bare hands!"

Taste

It is a given that a kid has to like the taste of a food in order for it to be among her favorites. For younger children, apple, grape, cherry, and chocolate are among the common, favorite flavors. But the unexpected flavor delight can be powerful, such as the irresistible blend of chocolate and peanut butter in a Reese's Peanut Butter Cup. Jelly Belly jelly beans fits the description as well. They are jelly beans in unusual flavors such as coconut, cantaloupe, chocolate pudding, and buttered popcorn. It is almost a game to throw a couple in your mouth, bite down, and then try to figure out what the various tastes are. You can also create flavors. The blend of pineapple and coconut, for example, creates pina colada—quite unexpected.

But few brands in the taste arena have the longevity of Baskin-Robbins. Irvine Robbins and Burton Baskin were brothers-in-law, as well as rivals with two ice-cream parlors. They decided to merge and create a diversity of flavors that soon became the trademark of Baskin-Robbins. In total, they have produced more than 700 flavors over the years. The continuous introduction of new taste sensations contributes to their longevity. Additionally, they have kept up-to-date with fads and trends with their product development and naming approach. For example, years ago they paid tribute to Beatlemania with a flavor called "Beatle Nut." The popularity of James Bond inspired "0031—Secret Bonded Flavor," not to mention varieties that cater to the health conscious looking for light and fat-free options. In this fashion, Baskin-Robbins has found a formula that has allowed them to survive for more than fifty years. They satisfy the timeless sweet tooth for those young and old but dress it up in a vast array of varieties, some tied to current trends and fads.

Currently, Baskin-Robbins products are enjoyed by more than 1.5 million customers a day around the world. Rivals abound, such as Haagen-Dazs and Ben & Jerry's, which can make Baskin-Robbins appear dated. But time and marketing acumen will ultimately decide which among these rivals can best apply the Ever-Cool formula.

Multiplicity

Some marketers have, all at once, added many sensory dimensions to their existing brands. Playskool, for example, introduced such software products as Mr. Potato Head Saves Veggie Valley. Once converted to computer software, such brands expand into sound and movement, along with varied visual experiences and even story development. Book publishers, too, have attempted to satisfy a child's many senses, as well as their minds, through the use of pop-ups, activities, and even sound chips. All of these added features compete for children's sensory attention as they meander through the bookstore. The added elements can help to build a deeper meaning for brands with a child, but only if executed in a way that truly touches a child's heart.

Some brands so mesmerize our multiple senses that we just sit and watch them in awe. One such brand began with Richard James, a marine engineer during World War II. One day, while stationed in Philadelphia's Cramp Shipyard, a torsion spring used in a testing meter fell off his desk and tumbled end over end across the floor while making an odd sound. Later that evening he said to his wife, "I think I can make a toy out of this." And he did. In fact, his wife Betty picked the name for the product and was instrumental in keeping this simple, yet engaging toy alive throughout the years. The toy, of course, is Slinky. It walks, which engages our sight. It makes a sound, which engages our ears. It is so unique in both that it engages our brain. More than 250 million have been sold. Slinky has become a piece of Americana.

Brand Challenges

- Can your existing brand surprise and delight a child by delivering an unexpected sensation, particularly in a category that does not cater to the senses?
- Can you create a new brand to do this?

9

Be Sensitive to Their "Age-tude"

They have bad manners and contempt for authority. They are ready
to contradict their parents, monopolize conversation in company,
eat gluttonously and tyrannize their teachers.
—Socrates (470?-399 B.C.)

A KID'S PSYCHE EVOLVES PREDICTABLY with time, and every couple of years there are dramatic shifts. This can be treacherous for the marketer because what might be cool for a
seven-year-old is considered babyish for the nine-year-old.
This has a dramatic impact on what, exactly, Ever-Cool is to
any specific target. Hence, it is critical to realize that designating an age target is not as important as designating an
attitude target. Too many marketing documents cite that
the target audience for this brand or that brand are kids
ages five to twelve. That is far too broad a description, and
it certainly does little to capture what kids are feeling on
the inside.

The Four Age-tudes

There are four general attitudinal stages ("age-tudes") of
a kid's psyche, the knowledge of which will make for a better marketing plan. The first age-tude I call the Parent-
Focused Kids. The second is the Gender-Focused Kids. The
third is the Transitional Tween. The fourth is the Turbulent
Teen. While all of these age-tudes may not be a kid

**You like the new look? Introducing my bear
formally known as Teddy . . . Madonna!**

marketer's specific audience, we will discuss all four because they are interrelated. Each stage flows sometimes gently, sometimes haphazardly, into the next. And each child sets his or her own pace. Knowing these four age-tudes will help the marketer create and maintain Ever-Cool brands.

PARENT-FOCUSED KIDS: *Parents, Dependence, Nurturing, Sensory, Growth*

Children of preschool age and younger depend upon their parents for almost everything. After all, kids come into the world void of any ability to fend for themselves, so they require constant care. Feeding and bathing and playing are all an important part of the first stage of life. Parents are also the key contact that a child has with the strange, enticing, and frightening universe. So it is not unusual that these younger children bond closely to parents, their protectors and guides to the world beyond. Security, comfort, and meeting basic physiological needs are paramount.

For those brands developed for the parent-focused kids, marketers often direct their communications toward parents since they are often the primary influencer. But as the parent-focused kids approach grade-school age, the shift begins, and these children begin to develop both brand preferences and the ability to articulate them, which often necessitates marketers shifting their communications directly to children. Regardless, the parent-focused kids have a few things in common.

Nurturing environments are important at this stage, and anytime a marketer can help enhance the bond from child to parent it can be very beneficial. Chuck E. Cheese's is an entertaining experience where a child and parent can go for a pizza meal and to enjoy games of all sorts. "We offer an experience where the family can interact," says Dick Huston, executive vice-president at Showbiz Pizza Time,

owners of Chuck E. Cheese's. It is a place "where parents
and kids can play games together, where parents can help
their children win, where they can all 'break bread.'" Such
places are early ventures out into the world for parent-
focused kids, always under the watchful eyes of parents who
introduce their children to new games and activities and
help them to understand the nature of these games, the
concept of winning, and the many ways to have fun. This
interaction brings parents and children together. This activity provides a bonding experience, a shared learning.

Characters introduced at this age are very nurturing in
nature as well, and some have gone on to be Ever-Cool with
this group because of the characters' ability to bond, to
teach, and to stay contemporary in their approach. The
purple dinosaur, Barney, fits this description. He is friendly,
nurturing, and seeks to help a child learn and grow in a
supportive environment. Barney has sold more than thirty
million videos, according to The Lyons Group. "Sesame
Street" and "Mister Rogers' Neighborhood" are two other
very important Ever-Cools for the parent-focused kids, and
they have achieved even greater success. They will be discussed in chapter 13, which focuses upon education and
learning.

For the parent-focused kid every experience is so new
and remarkable that the senses rule. He has to eat when he
is hungry. He has to have Mom when he is insecure. He has
to have that round, shiny, bouncing thing that Dad waves
past his eyeballs. So preschool toys are awash in bright, primary colors. Lights flash and bells ring. Objects of many
shapes and sizes provide tactile, learning experiences. The
Fisher-Price brand reigns supreme among these toys.
Discovery Zone FunCenter, which is an indoor entertainment and fitness facility, contains an obstacle course with
slides, tunnels, tubes, ball bins, swings, and more. Here the
muscles and the mind meet obstacles to overcome.

Because of their reliance on the overt senses and their

unsophisticated mental abilities, parent-focused kids are much more likely to respond to slapstick humor and not to satire or puns, which they simply won't "get." So when Bugs Bunny grabs Elmer Fudd and gives him a big, wet kiss on the nose, these kids will laugh and laugh. But they will not necessarily respond to Bugs Bunny's verbal bantering with Elmer, which can have a higher level of wit and sarcasm deemed cool by older kids.

As parent-focused kids start to venture beyond the parental grasp, particularly when they enter school, play-mates become increasingly important. Friends are new contacts to experience. Before grade school begins and for a short time there after, little boys continue to play with little girls, and that is just fine with both. Friendships are precious. Products and brands that help friends share experiences do well. A ball needs two people, as does a seesaw. Younger children are always on the lookout for either. Advertising directed at both sexes might fare well if both boys and girls are in the advertising, because boys and girls have yet to split into two quite different gender attitudes. But somewhere along the line, sexual identification dominates.

GENDER-FOCUSED KIDS: *Friends, Boyness, Girlness*

Around the time children enter grade school a strong sense of gender identity forms. They begin to develop closer attachments to same-gender friends. Boys begin to bond together, as do girls, into separate tribes. And these tribes taunt each other. As Nani, a seven-year-old girl, told us in focus groups, "Girls go to college to get more knowledge, boys go to Jupiter to get more stupider." They begin to like the same things that relate directly back to their innate psyche. The appeals that get their attention, and several of the Ever-Cool brands that capture them, were discussed in chapters 3 and 4.

Boys begin to test each other's physical strength. They

begin to see who can run the fastest and jump the highest. Power is the virtue. So is the skillful ability to gross someone out. They feel the need to demonstrate how tough they are. They become more hesitant to cry. These attitudes can begin to surface anywhere around ages five to six and last for several years. Clubs are important at this age, as is anything that says, "no girls welcome." Male action figures become hot! Videogames make their entrance and the games that emphasize sports or pit good against evil become popular for the first time.

Girls go through a similar process. They too begin to group together, to form social bonds connected by similar things they enjoy. Beauty becomes "cool," as do fashion, glamour, and the seeds of romance. Barbie dolls dominate. *The Baby-sitters Club* book series makes an entrance. Still, girls are not as anti-boys as boys are anti-girls, which is why if a brand during this stage appeals to both sexes, the rule of thumb is to include only boys in the commercial. Girls, says the rule of thumb, would not be turned off by seeing boys use the brand. But boys at this stage would be turned off by seeing girls use the brand.

In fact, it is during this gender-dominance stage where it becomes very tough to find a nonfood brand that appeals to both sexes; most are gender-specific. When it comes to the food category, however, brands are developed by taste appeal and typically by a theme that will not risk alienating either sex. Candy and cereal brands come to mind, and many have been successful. The opportunity, however, may be in generating foods that do, in fact, segment by gender. What would a boys-only brand of candy bar be like? Similarly, what would a girls-only brand of candy bar be like? By attempting to please both sexes, manufacturers may be missing opportunities to target each in creating new Ever-Cools. This will be explored in chapter 16.

THE TURBULENT TEEN: *Independence, Rebellion, Sexuality,*
   Identity

Before we discuss the Transitional Tween, it is important
that we first discuss the Turbulent Teen. Although this book
is not about the teen, per se, it is important to discuss teens
because they are an important point of reference for the
Transitional Tween.

First, allow me to begin by dispensing with a misconception. While the span of teen-age years (ages thirteen to
nineteen) has been around forever, some say the so-called
teen-age "attitude" has not been as exaggerated as we see it
today. By this, I am referring to those feelings associated
with independence, rebellion, sexuality, and the general
search for identity. But to truly understand this, we need to
delve back into history.

For virtually all of human existence, there were no formal schools or child labor laws. Once children grew to a
certain age, they learned their parents' vocation, whether
that be hunting, farming, crafts, or whatever. So the child
grew gradually into adulthood. By the time these "children"
were twelve or thirteen, they had a skill and the means to
employ it. Marriage happened early, and so too, did children. But with civilization came laws designed to educate
and protect our youth. These included compulsory education, marriage consent laws, child labor laws, and the like.
A conflict was, therefore, inevitable. Millions of years of
biology told teens it was their time to be independent, to
find a vocation, to marry, and to have children, but the
recent legal system said, "No. You have to wait. You're still a
kid." Yet the underlying aspirations and powerful yearnings
remain.

Hence, just when teen-agers are ready to venture forth
and be independent, our laws tell them they must remain
dependent. We are left with two forces on a collision
course. This has resulted in greater flashes of independence, rebellion, sexuality, and a search for identity that

can create conflict and angst between parents and their kids. While some sociologists claim that the existence of such conflict is greatly exaggerated, it is hard to convince a mother of that when her daughter comes home with a nose ring and purple hair.

The attitudes cited above mark the turbulent teen years. It is their age-tude. And marketers and performing artists have often captured teens with it. Adults who first saw Elvis Presley perform thought he was a bad influence on America's kids. "Why is he swinging his hips like that?" they would ask. Yet, teen-age girls loved it. The Beatles were also considered rebellious by adults for their music, their lyrics, their dress, and their "long hair," which by today's standards was not long at all. Madonna has been a master in conveying a rebellious attitude in the things she wears, in the things she says, and in the things she does.

MTV superbly unlocks the Ever-Cool formula among teens. First, MTV airs music videos that relate to a teen's age-tude. Rebellion, sexuality, and angst are common themes. Then, MTV continues to identify those up-and-coming performers who best represent these attitudes in the context of pop culture. This keeps MTV fresh. Additionally, the brand targets other parts of a teen's psyche. Since teens, for example, can define gross and bizarre in rather graphic terms, MTV introduced Beavis and Butt-head, two cartoon characters whose personas stretch the limits of crude. And so, MTV became a worldwide, Ever-Cool, mega-brand.

THE TRANSITIONAL TWEEN: *Kid, Teen, In-Between*

The Transitional Tween is caught, as the name implies, between two worlds. One is the gentle and fun-loving world of being a kid, the other is the angst-ridden world of being a teen. The transitional tween sees both places; he has a foot in each. One world provides the comfort of youth, the security of parents, and the *coolness* related to being a "boy" or "girl," while the upcoming teen world is a bit scary, yet strangely fascinating in an aspirational way: the music, the greater independence, the traces of rebellion, the opposite sex, the car! You can identify a transitional tween by visiting her bedroom, because she will have possessions from both worlds. Next to a stuffed Mickey Mouse doll, for example, you might find a pile of Madonna CDs.

These transitional tween years begin somewhere between ages eight and eleven. They last several years before the child is a full-fledged teen. Girls enter the tween years earlier and leave it sooner than boys do—their psyches are simply more mature. So, a ten-year-old girl will have much more in common with a twelve-year-old boy, attitudinally, than she will have with a boy of her same age. This is yet another factor that makes this group so tough to pin down demographically.

Because of all this, the transitional tween represents one of the greatest challenges for marketers. If you shoot too low and target the more kid-like emotions, then the tween will regard you as babyish. If you target too high and sound very teen-like with a good dose of satire, rebellion, or sexuality and the like, then you may be shooting way over the tween's head.

Testing in such situations is critical, for few brands have been able to consistently appeal to multiple segments. One successful example follows.

An Age-tude Ever-Cool

The Ever-Cool award must go to Nickelodeon for programming that runs up and down the age-tude scale, from parent-focused kids up to and sometimes past the transitional tweens. Programs such as "Rugrats" include both physical humor and nurturing elements appreciated by younger kids and a good dose of wit understood and appreciated by the older ones. A transitional tween can enjoy the more kid-like shows like "Doug," then tune into the more teen-like shows such as "Welcome Freshmen" and "All That." So the programs, in a very smart way, grow up as kids do. Importantly, Nickelodeon is considered cool by many kids because the programming is developed from a definite kid's perspective, and Nickelodeon is very astute at touching the many elements of kids' psyche mentioned earlier: power, control, the battling of fears, being gross, etc. "Nickelodeon accepts kids for what they are—from silly to serious," says Tom Harbeck, senior vice-president, Nickelodeon marketing and on-air promotion/creative director U.S. television. "We don't try to represent just one aspect of who they are."

This approach rubs off positively on the master brand of Nickelodeon. In 1995, according to one source, Nickelodeon reached nearly 25 million kids ages 2 to 11 each month. Of the top 100 ranked programs for kids ages 2 to 11, Nickelodeon accounted for 58 of them. To stay contemporary, Nickelodeon will "continue to grow with kids and remain relevant to their lives," says Mr. Harbeck. And they will "continue to ask the kids themselves about where they're going and what directions we should take." Nickelodeon is an Ever-Cool.

Brand Challenges

- Does your brand target a broad, vague age group, or does it zero in on a specific age-tude segment such as
  - Parent-Focused Kids?
  - Gender-Focused Kids?
  - Transitional Tweens?
  - Turbulent Teens?
- Does your brand reflect the attitude—the dimensions of cool—that is of most appeal to your primary target?
- Can you break the age-tude barrier and appeal to multiple segments without losing your brand's core strengths?

10

Understand Their Reference Groups' Connection to "Cool"

*There are three classes of friendship and enmity, since men
are so disposed to one another either by preference
or by need or through pleasure and pain.*
—Ptolemy (100-178)

IMAGINE YOU ARE AN EIGHT-YEAR-OLD BOY OR GIRL standing on the playground. Imagine that your feet are together, within a circle of chalk drawn around your feet. Now imagine that every time you try to step outside of the circle, one of your friends pushes you back inside, making it hard to get out, to try something new, to stand somewhere else. That's pressure exerted by your friend. And it impacts a child's evolving psyche.

PRESSURE: *The act of exerting steady weight or force against;*
bear down on

A kid experiments constantly, because that is what growing up is all about. But as a child experiments, he or she runs the risk that a friend or acquaintance will challenge the experiment with disapproval, or worse, a rebuke:

> "Why are you wearing *that* dress?"
> "Why do you like *that* music? Come on!"
> "Why are you playing with *Bobby?* He's stupid!"

And slap!—you are back within the circle of chalk, back where your friends feel more comfortable to have you, back

**Remember that time you asked if
Johnny told me to jump off a bridge would I do it?**

where they feel more comfortable about themselves. The parent-focused kid, that darling preschooler, does not wrestle with this pressure much, because her key point of reference is still her parents. But as school begins and greater contact with other children occurs, the point of reference begins to shift to those kids around her. Yet this pressure really comes from within, from a place where we, as individuals, need to belong, need to be accepted. These are powerful emotional desires that demand to be fulfilled. To be an outcast is frightening. And the child's desire to conform is evident in his ageless plea, "But Johnny's mother lets him do it." And every parent will counter with such ageless wisdom as, "If Johnny jumped off a bridge, would you?"

This chapter will answer several questions: What are the reference groups that ignite this pressure? Why are these kids in search of the illusive, mystic *cool?* And how can marketers leverage such knowledge to foster the Ever-Cool formula?

Reference Groups

The word *peer* is often used to designate those kids around the child who are of "equal" standing. Yet the word is actually a poor description of a child's associates, for the pressure that gets exerted can come from many different sources, and while some are often thought of as equals (friends), others are not viewed as such, for they may be older, more popular, or possess some other advantage in a child's eyes. In a kid's world, such things matter. The real issue, then, relates to defining the groups of kids around the child who provide a point of reference for him, and what implications that has for marketers.

Friends As a Point of Reference

Friends are a child's closest point of reference. They are the ones who share some common interests and attitudes, so they like to be around each other. A friend is comforting. A friend helps provide identity.

But friends come and go. Kids move. A new school year brings new friends. Such relationships are fragile. Every parent knows that Billy may be your son's best friend one week, and then an argument erupts and the friendship ends—for a day, week, or forever. Friendship is a dynamic process.

So kids are often searching for pals, someone to play with, someone to go places with. Many marketers have not only targeted the friendship circles that children have, they have also inspired them. Birthday parties are a ritual at Chuck E. Cheese's. Bring your friends around 11:00 A.M., play games, have a pizza, watch as the Chuck E. Cheese character (a person in a mouse suit) greets children and sings them a happy birthday song, and then you hit the road by 1:00 P.M. There is even a Chuck E. Cheese's birthday hotline in test markets. McDonald's offers birthday packages as well, as do many other eating establishments. Play areas have sprung up at many quick-service restaurants. They add a new dimension to the eating experience, that of social interaction and entertainment. And it is always more fun if you bring a friend along.

Who a kid picks as his friends also matters. *Newsweek* reported that a survey among twenty thousand high-school students revealed that the "kids that kids hang out with have the greatest influence on an adolescent's classroom performance." So friends can be important to a kid's entire future, which is why advertising campaigns to help stop illegal drug use have sometimes relied on friendships. Drug prevention advertising in the late 1980s asked kids to "be a real friend," and "if you know someone who's using drugs or thinking about using drugs, help that person say 'No.'" This helps drugs remain ever-*un*cool.

Friends are also a child's closest competitor. That is part of the fun. Friends compete to be line leader in class, they compete on tests, they compete in shows of physical strength and intelligence, they compete for the same toy, and later in life they may compete for the same boyfriend, girlfriend, job, salary, or riches. It never ends. One advertising campaign has used this notion of friend-competitor with great success. Kraft Foods markets both Post Fruity Pebbles cereal and Post Cocoa Pebbles cereal. The taste, shape, and colors have innate appeal to children. But Kraft Foods also buys the rights to the popular Flintstones characters, notably Fred and Barney from Hanna-Barbera, for use on packaging and advertising. In advertising, Barney tricks Fred out of his cereal. They are friends, yet competitors, true to kid relationships.

Aspirational Points of Reference

A child's frame of reference does not stop with those friends closest to him, nor does the pressure. The point of reference also encompasses many related groups. These include children who possess some attribute that the child desires; so, the child will watch them for tidbits of information.

Age References are those kids who are just a tad older. Five-year-olds wish they were seven. Seven-year-olds wish they were about ten. Ten-year-olds wish they were teens, and so it goes until that day comes when you wish you were younger. Age references may be a peer in terms of wealth, possessions, or whatever, but age is a big separator because with age comes greater independence. Older kids have a later bedtime. Older kids can go to the store by themselves. Older kids can _____ (fill in the blank). And younger kids watch them endlessly for cues on what is in and what is out.

Popular References are those kids who, by some standard, are considered to be the *popular* kids. They may be deemed as such because they have more friends; because they are more outgoing; or because they possess some physical, sporting, or personality trait that kids desire. Popular references are also under scrutiny by those who wish to be deemed popular themselves.

Wealth References are those who have more. They may be the same age, may be in the same class at school, may live on the same block, but they have something a given child wants. They may have the bigger house, more toys, the latest videogame, more freedom, a prettier appearance. They have more of some item that a given child lacks. They may not be a friend, but every kid knows who they are. They are the ones with more.

The Common Bond

All of these reference groups share one common bond. They all want to be *cool*. If they think they are already cool, then they will strive to retain it. If they do not think they are cool, they will strive to attain it. They will wear the clothes, see the films, buy the brands, play the sports, and listen to the music that they believe are cool. The hope is that, by mere association, they will be deemed cool also, which brings with the designation belonging, acceptance, and pride. This leads us to ask, what is this mystical thing called cool?

THE MYSTIC COOL: *Slang: Excellent, first rate*

Cool is in the eyes of the beholder. As noted in the last chapter, the definition of cool will vary by age because the psyche evolves over time. What the parent-focused kid thinks is cool will not be what the transitional tween thinks is cool, and so on. I have also noted in many focus groups that kids of even the same age-tude segment did not agree on what was cool. When children are asked to describe the cool kids, some will describe them as friendly, good at sports, and smart. Others will describe them as bullies, mean, snobby, showoffs, and dumb. It clearly depends on your own point of reference and whether you are on the inside looking out or the outside looking in. Defining cool is tricky, but there are some generalities we can discern.

Cool is whatever a kid likes and wants. If he does not like or want something, it is not cool.

Cool embodies what the psyche cherishes. Cheerleaders are often considered cool, as are football players. Each of them possesses an element that the psyche wants, such as beauty, strength, fame, or popularity.

Cool is often associated with an attitude. For example, there are Bart Simpson and Nickelodeon's Clarissa. Each of these characters is in control, confident, and savvy. They know the system, know the ropes, and know what is cool and what is not. If need be, they can outwit adults. This is not to say that all successful brands must have this same attitude, for many attitudes can be considered cool. It does mean that to be a long-term success, a brand will often have personality traits that help define its essence in a child's mind.

Cool is what you aspire towards. It would be cool to be older and more independent. It would be cool to be able to drive. It would be cool to attend a concert by a popular rock group. It would be cool to be a sky diver. It would be cool to be a professional athlete.

Cool often starts high and ends low. If a fad starts as high as with teens, it will spiral down to tweens, then to younger kids. Then it dies in the eyes of teens, because the last thing teens desire to be associated with is something that younger kids like, too. That would be babyish in the teen's eyes.

Cool is exclusionary. What you like is cool. What you obtain is cool. What the entire world finally has is no longer cool, because everyone has it. Part of cool is having something others do not. That makes a kid feel special. It is also the spark that drives kids to find the next cool item. No kid talks about last year's cool toy. They want what is cool this year, and they would love to be the first kid to get it.

Cool can be "the forbidden." As kids enter the tween and teen years, independence and rebellion raises its head. So cool can become those things you wish to do but parents will not allow. There is a broad range here, from the harmless stay-up-late debates to the not so harmless activities.

One New York City cab driver told me that he was sending his ten-year-old son back home to Guyana before it was "too late." He called peer pressure the "invisible force," that was beginning to influence his child in the wrong direction.

Cool is ever-changing. It is the "new, the current, the now!" It moves, rocks, rolls, and jerks, day-to-day, pushed forward by a ton of random acts: what music artist made the charts this week, what popular television programs were introduced in the fall season, what movie became a hit, what new male-action toy arrived from Japan at just the right time.

Cool is perishable. Here today, gone tomorrow as another new cool is born, unless the perishable is made Ever-Cool.

Cool cannot be predicted. No research report can tell you what brands will be cool next year. They can only tell you what is popular now. They can oftentimes tell you what new brands you are working on have potential to be cool, but until the baby is born and sent into the world, it is all educated guesswork. That is because you cannot tell what other brands will be introduced right before or after yours. The market makes up its mind in mysterious ways.

Cool can, however, be traced. A fashion becomes a hit because it is worn by a popular rock star. The rock star became a hit because his songs spoke of rebellion, romance, or worldly perplexities that bounced right off the eardrum and headed straight for a child's heart. Music is one of the first places kids look for cool.

Cool is profitable. Although it is an illusive entity, cool manifests itself in very concrete and profitable ways, which brings us to our next section.

How the Marketer Can Use Cool

A marketer's goal is to understand the nature of cool, and the reference groups that care about it, in order to impact the creation and long-term management of a brand.

Creating and Managing Cool

Because cool is something that a child likes, derived from what his psyche cherishes, marketers must begin the creation of an Ever-Cool by brilliantly addressing the child's psyche. That is what led to the introduction of brands such as Barbie, MONOPOLY, G.I. Joe, *Goosebumps,* and so many others that were discussed throughout Part II. This means hiring creative people whose offbeat talents can see a spectrum of color invisible to all others. These creative people understand the very heart of a child and can use that knowledge to create a movie, toy, or book series or a cereal that will fill the emotional need. Tools to help you create a new brand will be explained in chapter 16.

Because children seek cool attitudes, brands should strive to attain attitudes via depth of personality. Children can easily ascribe personality traits to Nike, Disney, McDonald's, and others. Such personality traits will vary, of course, depending on the nature of the brand and the emotional needs it satisfies. Importantly, this depth of personality is an aura that rises above mere product attributes and creates a strong bond between the child and the brand.

Because cool is aspirational and exclusionary, manufacturers should never oversupply the market with a brand, for such abundance makes the brand common, and thus *un* cool. It also upsets retailers stuck with too much product they cannot sell. The new Nintendo 64 was in scarce supply at Christmastime 1996. In early to mid-December, the 900,000 machines already shipped to stores were gone, which left frenzied parents to find bare shelves. Although such great scarcity was not Nintendo's intent (they were more worried about the risk of too much inventory), it could lead to tremendous sales in 1997, fueled by the multitude of kids who did not get the product, yet had to live in the shadow of the few who did.

Because children look to others for cues of coolness,

marketers should attempt to associate their brands with a child's associates, be they friends or aspirational points of reference. Advertisers insert kid actors in commercials, for example, who are at the high end of the audiences' age range, thus to associate their brands with older kids. This also helps extend the longevity of a brand as its appeal begins to spiral downward to younger kids.

Because kids strive to be with their friends, brands can be the conduits that bring a child's friends together, thus finding a role for itself within a child's larger world.

Because cool is ever-changing, perishable, and unpredictable, brands must always strive to remain contemporary by tying into trends and fads that children spark to, while never abandoning the need the brand satisfies, which is its reason for being. Finding the genesis of these trends and fads in a child's world and culture is important. This will be the emphasis of Part III.

Brand Challenges

- Can you identify your audience's reference groups?
- Do you know what they consider to be cool?
- Are you creating and managing cool as well as you might?

PART III
A Kid's World and Culture

A Kid's World and Culture

Part II discussed key emotional needs that reign eternal within a child's heart and how some marketers have satisfied them by creating brands that were launched in grocery stores, in toy aisles, on movie screens, on bookshelves, and elsewhere. In many cases, also highlighted were those brands that, through one fashion or another, have managed to survive beyond a couple seasons because they not only satisfied a timeless emotional need, but they also discovered a way to stay contemporary year after year by tying into trends or fads—the Ever-Cools.

Part III will take a closer, systematic look at a child's life via his changing world and culture, so the marketer can better understand the trends and fads that impact childhood needs. It also examines those aspects of a child's life that have not changed much over the years, for there are opportunities there as well. The insights gained can help the marketer create new brands and freshen existing ones. This broader knowledge of children will also allow the marketer to expand the role that a given brand plays in a child's life, thus creating a stronger, more enduring bond between the child and the brand.

Part III begins by reviewing such trends as a child's newfound awareness of the world (chapter 11), as well as his shifting family structure (chapter 12). Then we go on to examine the child's relationship with education (chapter 13) before dipping into his leisure activities (chapter 14), which is the birthplace of most fads. Finally, this section also reveals numerous everyday icons that, for one reason or another, hold special meaning for the child (chapter 15).

As with Part II, the purpose of Part III is to open the marketer's eyes to a kid's world as the child experiences it. This will help the marketer generate ideas that will touch a kid's heart.

11

Investigate Their
Newfound Awareness

If youth is a defect, it is one that we outgrow too soon.
—Robert Lowell (1917-1977)

KIDS ARE MORE AWARE of the world around them than at any time in history. They know more about foreign wars. They know more about a plethora of diseases. They know more about the rising crime rate. "Children in the nineties are growing up in times that are very different from those of their boomer parents," comments Joan Chiaramonte, vice-president of Roper Starch Worldwide. "AIDS, homelessness, kidnapping, and war occur in places that are, due to technology and media, no longer far-off and unreal."

This knowledge adds concerns to their lives, as is revealed in Exhibit #11-1. It shows that children ages eight to seventeen have concerns that are both broad and worldly and includes AIDS, kidnapping, drugs, crime, and pollution. These mimic some of the fears children cited in chapter 5.

AWARENESS: *Having knowledge; being conscious, cognizant*

It is easy to see why kids are more aware of the world around them. Efforts like Nickelodeon's "Nick News," a kids-directed news program, are plentiful. They serve up current events from a kid's perspective. The NBC network introduced a program called "News for Kids" that runs on

You go ahead and go shopping.
I'm going to organize a rally to help free Tibet
and stop global warming.

Exhibit #11-1

Concerns of Children Ages 8-17

AIDS
Kidnapping
Drugs
Homelessness
Neighborhood crime
Racial discrimination
Pollution
Divorce
Nuclear war
Having to fight a war
Amount of TV violence

Source: 1996 Roper Youth Report, rank ordered

Saturday mornings. It is also now common for broadcasters to create special reports to update children on specific events. One network, for example, developed a special broadcast directed to America's children to address their concerns regarding Desert Storm, the conflict with Iraq.

Even without the child-directed efforts, kids are more exposed to adult news programs. In the early 1960s, the average adult's weekly consumption of television newscasts was approximately 65 minutes. In the mid-1990s, it had grown to 330 minutes. As such, kids are more apt to be exposed to the news because their parents are watching it in an open forum, the living room, as opposed to discretely reading about it in the newspaper. So we should not be surprised when little seven-year-old Samantha asks her parents about the horrors of Bosnia. She simply overheard the 6:00 P.M. news as she was playing with her Barbie dolls.

Programming, as well, has had an impact in expanding a child's awareness. The July 13, 1996, issue of *TV Guide* compared television programming from the seventies to the programs of today. Back then, so noted *TV Guide,* Greg of "The Brady Bunch" feared telling the folks he wrecked the car. Today on "Mad About You," Paul's sister fears telling the folks she is a lesbian. Back then on "Happy Days," sharing some Coke meant sipping from the same glass. Today on "Beverly Hills 90210," sharing some coke means snorting some illegal substance. Even preschool-age children are apt to be exposed to adult-oriented material by being fed a daily diet of soap operas.

As children become more aware of the world around them, it affects the way they feel on many different levels. They can be enraged or saddened at the social injustices they witness or experience at home or abroad. They can be entranced and inspired by rich cultures of countries and peoples far away. They can feel the pride or discouragement of knowing where their country fits into the larger world order. In short, where there is a growing awareness of the world, budding emotional needs are not far behind.

The question is how the marketer can help satisfy such needs with either new or existing brands and to be Ever-Cool in the process. There are no easy answers, but there are very interesting examples of what some marketers have done across rather diverse categories.

The Environment/Pollution

As soon as the environment was viewed as a scarce resource in danger of depletion, Nature found a friend in the youth of the world. At the root of this effort lies a desire to nurture the earth and to nurture future generations that will benefit from what the earth has to offer. The past few decades have witnessed this growing trend, beginning out of the fiery decade of the 1960s. Kids care. And through the years, big business and uncaring governments are often cast as the villains who will rape the world for the sake of the dollar. Environmentalists, on the other hand, are cast as noble warriors for the planet (or alarmists, depending on your point of view).

Many manufacturers donate money or resources to environmental causes to demonstrate that the company is a responsible citizen. Many corporations will also work to reduce any harm that their manufacturing and marketing processes are doing to the environment. McDonald's, for example, eliminated polystyrene foam packaging in its U.S. restaurants. They also adopted strict policies for suppliers to guarantee that McDonald's does not purchase beef from rain forest or recently deforested rain forest land. When done well and responsibly, such efforts help develop a larger role for the brand in the child's life. That is a big statement, although kids may simplify those words by simply stating that McDonald's efforts are cool.

One of the most creative concepts born of this environmental trend was the animated kids program of "Captain Planet and the Planeteers," created by the Turner Broadcasting System in 1989 and debuted in 1990. Each of four of the five planeteers represents one of the earth's four elements: Earth, Fire, Water, and Wind. The fifth planeteer represents the power of the Heart, which symbolizes compassion for the earth. The planeteers direct their special powers to save the world from environmental villains. When the planeteers join their powers, they call forth Captain Planet, and together they fight evil forces that would do harm to the environment. Such evil is embodied in characters such as Verminous Skumm, who spreads filth and disease, and Duke Nukem, who loves radioactivity. The program is a nice combination of a current trend or concern tied back into a kid's emotional psyche that desires control, power, and an entertaining good-versus-evil story. "Captain Planet" teaches that every individual must respect planet earth and preserve its resources if we are to survive.

"Captain Planet," however, is based on a "current" kid trend, which means it will stay Ever-Cool only as long as the environment stays near the top of a kid's mental list relative to other trends and fads in television programming that draw a kid's attention.

Crime

As crime reaches us in the news, in our neighborhoods and in our lives, children grow more concerned and more afraid. Those efforts that protect a child from crime, allay a child's fears of crime, or even use a crime as a theme in a fanciful story, can be successful.

Many crime preventive, safety-oriented products target parents directly. Some are worth pointing out even though the focus of this text is upon generating a child's request. One such product is an electronic device that sounds an alarm should a child stray more than fifteen feet from his parent. Another is Ident-A-Kid Services of America. They provide a laminated, photo ID card that includes a description of the child, a picture, a thumb print, and an address, should the child become lost. Additionally, the Internet is filled with advice and services for parents to help them provide a safer environment for their children. One is called Safe-T-Child Online. It offers parents the knowledge they need to help prevent their children from becoming lost, abducted, molested, or abused. As crime becomes more prevalent, so too will these products and services.

As cited earlier, brands have been created to help a child feel safer. Mattel's My Watch Dog was a toy that automatically barked when an intruder (usually another family member) would enter the child's room. It allowed the preschooler to feel just a bit more at ease. Brands such as

Huglight Mickey and Gloworm have done the same. Such brands will continue to be in need.

Additionally, crime and criminals have always been used to spin stories for novels and films. Sherlock Holmes has his Professor Moriarty. Batman has his Joker. Fanciful criminals are wonderful villains to thwart. And recently a new concept was born within this arena. Her name is Carmen Sandiego, a villainous character in a game called Where in the World Is Carmen Sandiego? Players pit their sleuthing skills against Carmen and her fellow criminals, and with the help of encyclopedias and atlases, each player attempts to locate the criminals hiding somewhere in the world. In effect, a child learns about the world while trying to stop Carmen from continuing her life of crime. The game makes a child feel mastery, power, and the triumph of good over evil. It is a blend of a child's awareness, a fanciful story, a piece of a child's psyche, and a geography lesson all rolled into one.

War

The more a child hears of wars, the greater concern he will have. And it is very hard to imagine how such a devastating concept of war can be used to ignite a child's passions for fun. But that was the success of the 1983 film *WarGames*. It starred Matthew Broderick as David, a teenage computer hacker who hacks his way into a classified military computer system. In so doing, he inadvertently begins a countdown toward global thermonuclear war. But he is also the only person alive who can stop the countdown by using the same computer skills that got him into trouble in the first place. Imagine: a kid begins a war, and a kid prevents one—very suspenseful. The film tied into several trends at the time, such as the emergence of videogames, computers, and the arms race. It then added all the essential ingredients that kids love: mastery, power, control over adults, danger, and the conquering of fear, all served up brilliantly. It was the fourth-largest box-office hit that year.

One promotional approach to world peace began with The Barbie Children's Summit Month developed by Mattel in 1990. The event brought girls from countries around the world to meet in New York City to discuss world issues. Children at the meeting were to decide which worthwhile cause was of most concern, and then Mattel was to donate money from each Barbie doll sold in a given period for that cause. World peace was the winning issue, and Mattel donated a half-million dollars to the Carter Center in Atlanta to be used to that end. Mattel took a responsible path, and the promotion had the added benefit of helping Barbie, the brand, look and feel contemporary, thus perpetuating Ever-Cool.

Diversity

Children in the United States reflect a great ethnic mix. The original Baby Boom was 75 percent non-Hispanic white according to Census Bureau estimates. The next baby boom is only 67 percent non-Hispanic white; 15 percent black; 14 percent Hispanic; and the rest a mix of Asian, American Indian, Eskimo, and Aleut. Concentrations of ethnic groups are greater in certain cities such as Los Angeles, in which grade-school children are predominantly of Hispanic descent. There is pride in this individual origin, and ethnic groups are striving to preserve their unique differences rather than becoming lost in the melting pot. Increasingly, marketers are targeting children not only by age and gender, but also by ethnic composition. They are recognizing the richness of diversity.

Disney introduced *Pocahontas* and *Aladdin*. Doll manufacturers create dolls of many ethnic origins. "Captain Planet's" planeteers are drawn from different ethnic groups across the world. Manufacturers also develop advertising campaigns directed toward ethnic groups, tailored to their language and to the role that the specific brand plays in their cultural lives.

But it is important to realize that the timeless truths that exist in a child's heart, independent of his diversity, remains constant. In an Ogilvy & Mather kid study conducted around the world, some twenty Ogilvy & Mather offices reported a slew of the same popular brands including Disney, MTV, and Nike. Such brands transcend borders because they target a common, universal element of a child's psyche. MTV, for example, has done so much to unite the youth of Europe through music, some claim that teen-agers throughout the many countries of Europe have more in common with each other than they do with their own parents.

Peter Pan Syndrome

With so much turbulence in the world, and a child's greater exposure to it, we have also heard many children recently say that they would prefer to stay a child for a while longer. The lyrics to Toys 'R' Us advertising ties right into this theme: "I don't want to grow up 'cause if I did, I wouldn't be a Toys 'R' Us kid." That is very much in keeping with the times. Chuck E. Cheese's tagline of "Where a Kid Can Be a Kid" appeals to that feeling as well. It is not surprising that the 1995 Zandl Report discovered that a child's favorite place to be is at home. This was not only the number-one choice among eight to twelve-years-olds, but it applies to teen-agers as well. Kids want to be kids more than ever, it seems. If the world looks too uninviting, then they will stay home.

Brand Challenges

- How can you embrace a child's newfound awareness?
- Can you create a new brand based upon issues and needs related to the environment, crime, war, and others?
- Can you use such issues to develop promotions for existing brands, thus to be corporately responsible while fostering Ever-Cool?

No, my mom isn't home. Would you like to speak to my alternate-lifestyle-nonbirth parent?

12

Understand Their
Shifting Family Structure

The strength of a nation is derived from the integrity of its homes.
—Confucius (551-479 B.C.)

FROM A DISTANCE, ALL LOOKS CALM on our planet. If tracked over eons, this sphere would show little change as it steadily revolves around its rather common star, in a sleepy solar system, in a relatively empty quadrant, in an unexplored universe.

But that is not where children really live, for that universe, solar system, and even most of that planet are far too immense to be of day-to-day importance to their existence. Instead, a child's universe is a town. His solar system is a block filled with a row of houses, each of which is a planet unto its own with its unique rules and inhabitants. And each planet comes with a door, some windows, an assortment of living, breathing creatures, and a planetary code of behavior created by adults for the obedience of all (or so they say). . . . Some call this home.

FAMILY: *All the people living in the same house*

This household planet is vital for the child, for it is the center from which most things spring, like the laws of behavior, like the seeds of learning and discovery, like the experiences that shape the foundation of world perceptions. Unfortunately, many things can change quickly in a

137

household, leading to uncertainty and confusion. The inhabitants grow. Relationships shift. Parents divorce. People move to new neighborhoods. Sometimes these changes are welcomed and sometimes they are not. Regardless, such shifts can create an emotional need within the child that in turn will demand fulfillment.

This chapter is about a child's household planet and about some of the key changes taking place, as well as some things that never seem to change. Each can lead to opportunities for the observant marketer to help create a brand, freshen an existing one, or enhance the bond a brand has with the child.

The Things That Are Changing

Kids are expected to grow up faster. Today, some 26 percent of households with children under 18 have only a mother at home, and 4 percent have only a father. Additionally, 70 percent of moms work full- or part-time, leaving the child to spend his time in daycare or to come home to an empty house. Today's children are often responsible for tasks not expected of the previous generation of kids. They cook and clean more often. And they shop. One study revealed that over the past decade, the number of children shopping for the family's groceries has doubled. Marketers of even adult brands must ask themselves if they are really reaching all of their influential audiences.

Kids have a greater need to be and feel safer. Some children leave for school long after a parent has already left for work. Some kids come home from school before the parent arrives. These situations create a need for added safety as outlined in chapter 11 and have already spawned the growth of day-care centers, home alarms, and even beepers. Products such as these will continue. The day will come when children will be tracked by satellite in the same fashion that today's cars can be tracked by companies such as LoJack, a service capable of pinpointing a stolen car's exact location by use of silent homing signals transmitted by the car itself.

Kids have a greater need for family. As families become separated by the nature of our evolving society, kids have a greater need for the bonds that family provides. In survey after survey, kids continue to say that family is vital to them. And although it may come as a surprise to many, kids still continue to list parents as their role models (although few will admit it to their parents). Importantly, in the face of a high divorce rate and dual-income families, which can separate parents from children, many parents are striving harder than ever to maintain the bond with their kids. This is a trend in itself, and it has helped fuel the growth in kid marketing. "I believe the real change in the American family," stated Rena Karl, executive editor of *The Marketing to KIDS Report*, "came about due to better parenting and a stronger effort by parents to "do right' by their kids. Families are more democratic. There is more communication, discussion and respect between kids and parents. Parents read more about better discipline and they talk to each other about becoming better parents. A greater number of divorcing parents go through counseling and make an effort to spare their kids some of the trauma of a disrupted household."

Grandparents play a growing role. In a flashback to another time, grandparents are on the comeback trail. As single, working, and divorced parents become more prevalent, grandparents shoot in to help with the grandchild's upbringing. According to *American Demographics*, "an estimated 2.3 million American children under the age of 15 were cared for by a grandparent in 1993 while their mothers worked." That is up from 1.8 million in 1988. In a Roper Starch Worldwide study, also cited in *American Demographics*, U.S. grandparents estimate that they spent a median of $400 per year on their grandchildren. As any parent will tell you, grandparents are desperate to connect with their grandkids. And since expenses such as home mortgages are already often paid for, grandparents have more discretionary dollars to spend. This is big marketing muscle. Marketers must take notice.

Implications

Marketers who can fill needs created by this shifting household structure will reap the benefits. Some products, for instance, bring the family closer. They act as conduits between parents and their children and lead to a greater bond that fills the need for togetherness. Electric trains have forever been purchased for sons, then played with by both father and son, side by side. Many parents play videogames with their children. Such products provide an opportunity to "share" in the experience. Nickelodeon's program "Family Double Dare" pits one family against the next, each of which must work together as a team to win. Films can also allow children and their parents to share experiences. Disney, as mentioned earlier, is so adept at touching the childlike emotions that live in all of us, that kids and parents flock to see the films together. In this way, they create common memories. Films like *Batman* and *Casper* use a nostalgic bent that directly appeals to the parents' memories of childhood while using updated action and storylines to appeal to the child. That makes the movies cool for the baby boomers and cool for their kids.

Successful programming has reflected the shift in the family structure over the years and have included such shows as "One Day at a Time" (divorced mother), "Step By Step" (remarriage), and "Full House" (widower and extended family). Each touched a child's heart by demonstrating that such families cannot only survive, but do so successfully, which denotes achievement, belonging, and love.

Once again, some brands recognize a parent's need to

safeguard their children. One service called KidCalls Telephone Monitoring Service is designed for the "latchkey kid." At a specified time each day when the child should be home, an automated calling system phones home and asks the child to respond by pressing certain phone keys. If any trouble is indicated, the parents and others can be called.

Still, other ideas are conceived out of the notion that children can take care of themselves. *The Karate Kid* was a film about a boy who desperately needed to defend himself against bullies, and he found a father-figure, in the form of a martial arts expert, to train him. The film dipped deep down into a child's psyche and touched a cord that all kids feel, made more relevant by the increase in crime among youth. And not surprisingly, martial arts schools catering to children have exploded over the past few decades; many kids consider them to be cool. These schools fit a growing need children have to take care of themselves.

Because a child's life can change dramatically from one day to the next, McDonald's has attempted to help both the child and his parents cope. Ronald McDonald House Charities is one such example. It provides a "home-away-from-home" for families of seriously ill children being treated at nearby hospitals. The program has more than 165 houses in 12 countries. McDonald's also partners with the American Red Cross to provide relief to thousands of families affected by natural disasters. Clearly, McDonald's, the brand, is far more than a burger and fries.

In the end, marketers must ask themselves how their brands can fit into a child's changing household structure, in order to touch the child's heart in deep, everlasting ways.

The Things That Stay the Same

While some things are changing on a child's household planet, other things have stayed the same. These constants cannot be forgotten because they, too, give the marketer more fodder for both understanding kids and for using that knowledge to generate ideas to help brands look and feel cool.

Parents

A parent, for most children, is a constant and is at the very center of a child's universe. There is no other inhabitant of the household planet who has such a vast role and relationship with a child. And interestingly, parents actually play many roles.

In the early years of a child's infancy and preschool, parents are protectors and comforters. They provide the care and warmth in a world where much anxiety can be resolved with a cozy hug. Nightmares vanish with a mere trip to Mom's bedside, and a boo-boo can be eased with a tender kiss and a emphatic "there, there." Parents are also teachers and wise men, seemingly possessing the vast stores of universal knowledge that comes in handy at homework time. The parent-as-friend arises whenever the child shares a precious moment together with a parent, either when confiding, playing, or joking.

Very early on, children also soon discover that parents are the makers-of-rules. With a parent in that role, a young child can feel comforted that there are, in fact, codes of conduct. Understanding what is right and what is wrong sets the groundwork for behavior, reward, and punishment. As long as a child knows the rules, he knows how to behave in order to live happily on his household planet. But as the child gets older, the rules become confining, especially as a child yearns for greater independence. This is when the maker-of-rules becomes the resident dictator, that household ruler who nags the child to do his homework, to pick up his clothes, to eat with her mouth closed, to take out the trash, to buy this and not that, and issues a thousand other demands.

But all is not lost, for most children recognize that their parents can be heroes when they ride to the rescue with a bandage or with needed advice. They are transports when children need rides to visit friends and to go to parties. Mom and Dad are also deemed the ultimate resource, for they often seem to come through with enough cash to pay for a movie, toy, or candy bar when need be. But despite these moments of being heroes, resources, or comforts and such, parents are also a child's competitor, for there's nothing more a child loves than to beat Mom or Dad in whatever game possible. After all, to beat the maker-of-rules is a special moment, one to be cherished.

Marketers who happen to be parents see it all every night when they return home from work. "To my five-year-old Robbie, I've finally emerged as his pal," says Rick Roth, executive group director of worldwide client service at Ogilvy & Mather New York. "To my seven-year-old Willie I'm lots of things—a competitor he has to beat, a teacher who instructs him on how to win, and the man he wants to be when he grows up. To my fourteen-year-old daughter Jennie, I have suddenly gone from Daddy as hero to the adult who just does not understand."

Knowing the roles a parent can play, and has played for eons, can help the marketer generate ideas that appeal to a child's heart. Some marketers, for example, may ensure that a parent is depicted in a commercial for a preschool product to denote comfort and security for the viewing child. Other marketers may provide information to the child about a brand's safety or nutritional advantages in order to arm him with valuable information about the brand should the parent be in the role of dictator (i.e., gatekeeper). Learning aids are ever-present at book stores to appeal to parents in their role as teachers and wise men. Bart Simpson will beat his dad Homer time and again. And when he does, Dad as competitor is vanquished. That is cool.

Siblings

Another constant on a child's household planet is the sibling. In its August 1996 issue *American Demographics* reported that "the relationships people share with siblings are often the longest-lasting they will ever have. Siblings are there from the beginning, and they are often still around after parents, and even spouses and children, are gone." But the past several decades of divorce and remarriages have shifted the standard sibling dynamics. Stepparents, stepbrothers and stepsisters, and half-brothers and half-sisters are common. This adds complexity to the family structure. Still, some family dynamics stay the same.

Although siblings can share much love, they will also compete on almost every level. They compete for a parent's affection. Siblings of the same sex will compete for each other's toys and other possessions, given that they often like similar items. They also compete for neighborhood friends and eventually for girlfriends and boyfriends. The television series "Sister, Sister" is an excellent example of such rivalry, born out of reality.

A child's perception of his sibling is also very dependent on each child's sex and age. Brothers think sisters are, well, silly girls. Sisters think brothers are gross, which they are. So commercials for slimy products might depict brothers grossing out their sisters. Younger siblings look up to older ones and often want to emulate them. Older siblings want little or nothing to do with the younger ones and are thrown into a tizzy if they are asked to watch after them. This has been the way of things for centuries, and it is likely to remain the same for many more. *American Demographics* reports that the oldest siblings tend to be authoritative, middle siblings the mediators, and youngest siblings the free-spirited ones. Although these descriptions are merely generalities, these insights have made for many films and television program episodes.

Pets

In fact, the only living creature that seems to be free of conflict on this household planet is the family pet. Yes, dogs, cats, turtles, fish, birds, and hamsters have always had a neutral position. That is their strong suit. They give love and affection, take the same in return, and stay clear of all the politics. And in so doing, they play a valuable role as confidant and lifelong friend and protector. This is the ageless appeal of *Lassie,* the story of a dog that captured the hearts of generations. Whenever a problem arose, Lassie was there to save the day. Pets have always been a focus of stories and playthings.

You do not even have to worry about where a pet turtle ranks in the family hierarchy. Just feed the darn thing, watch him paddle about, and if you are ever sent to your room for violating the dictator, you can look deep into the turtle bowl and tell your friend your side of things, and he will listen. Then add a touch of imagination, a bit of transformation, an ounce of strength and power, a dab of good vanquishing evil, and you can imagine that your pet turtle is nothing less than a Teenage Mutant Ninja Turtle, the popular characters that made their way from action figures to movies to pillowcases. How else can such a common household pet become such a wonder, if not by adding all those precious elements of a child's psyche mentioned earlier? Legend has it that the concept began as a rough drawing on a cocktail napkin more than a decade ago and soon turned into cool warriors in the personalities of Donatello, Leonardo, Michaelangelo, and Raphael. This is the same lesson discussed earlier: take the common and make it special. Find a trend or a constant, and envelop it in a child's psyche.

A marketer, then, can generate new ideas by looking inward at the family, their changes, their interactions, their constants, their needs. He can even take something as common as a household pet and transform it into something wondrous by applying the elements that delight a child's heart.

A Family Ever-Cool

Some Ever-Cools weave themselves into the fabric of a family's life, in ways we do not often stop and think about.

McDonald's is one of these Ever-Cools. McDonald's provides food, a basic necessity, and it does that quickly, which fits into a family's busy life-style. In fact, 8 percent of the American population visits McDonald's on an average day. Ninety-six percent of the U.S. population has visited a McDonald's at least once. It stays cool among kids, in part, by providing a Happy Meal packed with contemporary playthings.

But McDonald's also recognizes a child's broader life, and his and her family's, and provides charities and aid to those in need while trying to be responsible to the environment. Some might say all this is self-serving, yet, McDonald's does it nonetheless, in the attempt to be a good corporate citizen and a good consumer brand. McDonald's is also one of the largest employers of youth in America, having employed older kids, their brothers, their sisters, their friends, not to mention their parents and their grandparents. McDonald's, the brand, has become a part of the family in many ways.

Says Paul Schrage, senior executive vice-president and chief marketing officer for McDonald's, "McDonald's captures children's hearts by really understanding them and knowing what's important to them. McDonald's treats children with the respect they deserve." They plan to stay a part of a child's life by "doing our homework and always staying on top of what's important to children and their parents." They offer food, convenience, playthings, aid, and jobs—quite an Ever-Cool.

Brand Challenges

- How can your brand play a role in a child's family in order to create a relationship in deep, everlasting ways?

- Can you generate a new brand idea that takes into account the things that stay the same, and the things that shift, on a child's household planet?

13

Find Opportunities in Their Educational Arena

Personally, I'm always ready to learn,
although I do not always like being taught.
—Winston Churchill

"BILLY!" HIS MOM SCREAMS for the third time from downstairs. "Time to wake up for school. You're going to be late again!"

The impatient, irritated sound of his mother's voice finally penetrates Billy's consciousness, just enough to invade his dream of winning an Olympic gold medal in pole vaulting. The stark, beckoning voice jerks his mind upward past the cheering crowd, past yet a hundred other fantasies just begging to be fulfilled, and up toward a foggy recognition of the real world. As Billy's body moves ever so slightly, that first telltale sign of waking, a helpless realization sinks the pride and achievement that the dream provided. "You're only 10," thinks Billy, "you have never even tried pole vaulting, and worse, it's Monday, the worst day of the week." The next five days are nothing less than hurdles to be overcome until a hundred dreamed-up activities can be his for the taking. Or at the very least, he will be able to sleep late. What Billy does not know is that his mom and dad probably felt the same just thirty minutes before as they rose from their slumber to face five more days of work.

"Monday," Billy thinks as his eyes open and are stabbed

I hope the next software upgrade will have
Dissect A Principal on it.

by the rays of light beaming past curtains his mother must have opened in a vain attempt to wake him up. "Oh, man," Billy sighs.

"Billy!" his mother shouts again from downstairs, and then she shakes her head. "Oh, man."

EDUCATION: *The act or process of imparting or acquiring general knowledge and of developing the powers of reasoning and judgment*

Life for a child happens roughly in thirds. About a third is devoted to leisure and play; a third to sleeping (although some parents would swear that it is much more); and a third to education, both school and homework.

Education incites many emotions—from sadness to pride, from frustration to achievement. Because of these emotions it brings forth, it is a fertile ground for creating new brands or contemporizing established ones that foster the positive emotions and resolve the negative ones.

But a kid's educational life is so vast a subject, it is best to break it down into a couple of components so that each can be discussed. I have chosen two areas to review: making education engaging and finding marketing opportunities in the course of the schoolday itself. Ideas for products and services can come from either arena, constrained only by the sharpness of our insights and the limits of our imagination. Once again, I have included examples of what some marketers have done to fulfill a child's emotional needs.

Making Education Engaging

Children love to learn, for the act of gaining knowledge about the world and discovering new horizons elicits so many positive emotions; children take comfort in knowing how the world works, because that can make it a less frightening place. As children learn, they can take pride in an accomplishment and the mastering of a skill. This combines with the feeling of advancing, getting smarter, getting older, and being more mature. Every time a child wins a gold star from a teacher for getting an A on a spelling test, it is a big deal. To be recognized for achievement is important, because it feeds self-esteem.

Educators agree that kids learn best when they are excited by what they are learning. Unfortunately, that cannot happen unless the material to be learned is served up in an exciting and entertaining way. Those who can excite and entertain will reap the benefits, but they must first understand what "exciting and entertaining" means to the child. Simply, it means engaging the psyche!

Math Blaster was the most popular math software program for young children in the United States in 1995. It was created by Jan Davidson, who managed to combine "the addictiveness of computer games with an educational lesson plan," according to *People Magazine*. The program kept a child's interest in solving equations while "helping a tiny green Blasternaut zap villainous outer-space invaders." Davidson, in essence, used a good versus evil storyline, dressed up in a contemporary way, to engage a child's psyche. The combination of education and entertainment worked. Sales in 1995 of Davidson's educational software company were $148 million. Will Math Blaster become an Ever-Cool? Well, that depends on what Davidson can do to keep it contemporary year after year vis-à-vis product upgrades and promotional opportunities.

Sylvia Branzei, a schoolteacher in California, also desired to educate kids, but she targeted a different part of the child's psyche to get their attention. She wrote a book entitled *Grossology*. It contains answers to rather gross questions about the human body such as "what are zits made of?" and "why do I barf?" It grabs a child's interest and teaches him a bit about the physiology in the process. According to one source, the book came out in November of 1995 and by Christmas had sold 25,000 copies. Kids must have been engaged.

"Engagement" can also be achieved by way of a reward. Pizza Hut, for example, offered grade-school kids free pizza for reading a certain number of minutes each day during the summer months. Does such a promotion help Pizza Hut look and feel cool? You bet it does. Pizza Hut involved itself in an important part of a child's life.

Reader Rabbit's Interactive Reading Journey, a CD-ROM–based reading program for children three to six, has some 40 books within it. Each book is quite short, with only about 20 pages apiece and about 3 to 10 words per page, which makes each relatively easy to master. Yet each book is also slightly more challenging than the last. And each time a child finishes one, he or she feels the thrill of accomplishment. And when the child finishes each set of eight books, he passes through a "gate" and into another land of eight more, and so on until he reaches the end of the journey, book 40.

The constant feeling of mastery that comes with accomplishing each short book and passing through each gate is vital, for it inspires pride and keeps the child interested. The Learning Company, makers of Reader Rabbit products, must have taken its cue from videogame manufacturers who construct games with many levels so that the child will be constantly challenged with progressively harder stages. *Reader Rabbit's Interactive Reading Journey* is also an evolution from the earlier, simpler Reader Rabbit products. Its evolution has helped it remain in the public eye.

Some parents take the responsibility of teaching completely into their own hands. The National Home Education Research Institute (NHERI) believes that there are up to one million students in kindergarten through twelfth grade who are being home schooled. Home schooling is based upon the belief that a child's natural curiosity and parental guidance would prove more effective than traditional methods. Alan Castro saw an opportunity in this and opened up E Land, a retail store with texts and supplies for home schoolers, as reported in the Fall 1995 *Big Blue Box*. The *E* stands for entertain, educate, and evolve. We can expect more and more marketers to target this growing market, thus helping the parent become an effective teacher by engaging a child's interest.

There are two prominent Ever-Cools within the educational category. Both appear when the child is young. One is "Mister Rogers' Neighborhood." It is the longest-running children's program on public television, says one source, with more than six hundred half-hour shows in its library. Importantly, the television program is one about feelings—"about love, fear, sadness, jealously, anger, friendship, trust, joy, and satisfaction." By focusing on childhood emotions, the show helps children understand more about themselves—which promotes self-esteem. To keep it contemporary, "Mister Rogers' Neighborhood" invites interesting guests, visits interesting places, and confronts current issues such as divorce.

And then there is "Sesame Street," whose mission is simply to help children learn, and it has. Children's Television Workshop, who launched "Sesame Street," has become the largest single teacher of young children in the world, having helped educate more than 120 million children in some 130 nations over the years. The series has also achieved 58 Emmys. Its secret: the unique blend of education and entertainment that reflects a child's needs, interests, and preferences. Plus, Children's Television Workshop continually adapts their curriculum goals and introduces new television techniques based upon research that tells them what children "continue to need, understand, and find engaging." This sounds like another Ever-Cool.

Concurrently, there is another mega kids' brand waiting in the wings, tiptoeing near the educational arena—Disney. The top "edutainment" software products already carry Disney themes (e.g., *The Lion King* and *Pocahontas*). But they are just a breath of what could be. Says Kenton Low, vice-president of marketing and sales at Disney Educational Publishing, "For kids to grow and contribute in a twenty-first century environment, they need engaging experiences that inspire curiosity and encourage them to believe in the power of their own minds. With these experiences, a whole child emerges, full of self-confidence and the ability to make decisions and solve problems in any kind of situation." Although Mr. Low would not comment about the specific learning products under development, the depth and breadth of his vision is all encompassing. If any brand can serve learning on a platter of excitement and engagement, it would be Disney. They have but to aggressively enter the educational arena.

The Schoolday

School has not changed much in recent years. Oh, things have been added, things deleted, hours changed, different ideas about education have been attempted, but the basic structure has remained pretty constant. School is in session roughly 180 days a year. It begins in September and continues through the first or second week of June (unless the school is on a year-round program). Reading, writing, and math, with ventures into science and social studies, are the main courses as they have been for many years. Each day begins at about 8:30 A.M. and goes until about 3:30 P.M., with standard breaks for lunch and recess.

Some marketers have found needs to be fulfilled in this schoolday structure, but you can only find them if you dissect the day itself. Some opportunities help parents, some target kids, some target both.

Morning: Most kids are awakened by their parents, they stumble out of bed, wash up, and put on their school clothes. The rush is on and nerves are thin. The kids eat breakfast, which they typically select. Some kids might watch a bit of television. Mom or Dad assembles the child's lunch and throws it into a bag or lunch box as they,

themselves, scurry about to get ready for work. Or perhaps
the parent just gives the child enough change to buy lunch
in the school cafeteria. Then, as the child carries a back-
pack of folders and books, and the parents juggle a brief-
case and/or lunch pails of their own, the family makes a
disorderly dash to the family car, from which the child will
either be dropped off at school or at a school bus stop.

In this seemingly insignificant but hectic ritual alone,
marketers have found plenty of needs to fulfill. Here are
three: Oscar Mayer introduced Lunchables lunch combinations, a prepackaged lunch that parents can simply throw
into a lunch bag, thus saving time and parental headaches
that arise in the pre-dawn madness of getting the kids ready
for school. A Lunchables lunch combination includes a balanced meal of a meat, a cheese, crackers, a drink, and a
treat such as pudding or candy bar—just the thing to
inspire a child's request. Another example that fulfills a
need is Kids on the Go. It is a taxi service in Fishkill, New
York, reports *Youth Markets ALERT,* that gives kids a lift to
school because their parents work and cannot find the time
to drive them to school. Even Post Alpha-Bits cereal is a
brand born from a simple education-related idea: give kids
a breakfast cereal in letter shapes that they can use to practice spelling words. The brand is not only challenging, but
it allows a child to use his imagination. All of these ideas
seem quite simple, but they each required someone to dissect the family's life and spot an interesting need.

Arrival: The children arrive at school, play a while as they
wait for the bell to ring, then are escorted into class where
they stow their books and jackets. They gaze at each other
intently, looking at new clothes, new shoes, new friends, etc.
The pressure abounds. One lesson after another follows as
the students sit facing the front of the classroom, or in study
circles, as a teacher guides them through science, math,
English, history, and such. Maps are about the walls, as are
past assignments that achieved merit in the teacher's eyes.

Some marketers help the child "achieve" in the classroom itself. Chrysler Corporation sponsored the National Geography Bee, which reached some 6 million students and 12 million parents, according to *Youth Markets ALERT.* Chrysler received exposure via logoed maps sent to schools and were identified as the sponsor at the bee's national finals on PBS. Apple Computer donated computers to the classroom and recently began a program to help teach parents to use computers as well.

Lunch: The bell rings and the children form lines to go to lunch, where they gobble down their packed lunch or buy lunch from the school's cafeteria. The faster they eat, the more time they will have on the playground before the lunch period is over.

Licensees have covered lunch pails with the likenesses of a thousand characters, from Batman to Pocahontas, so kids can be assured of having the "right" character who will reflect their preferences to all onlookers. Some kids pull their Oscar Mayer Lunchables out of their bags and begin to snack. Some drink Capri Sun, a single-serving juice drink whose foil pouch signals *cool.* Said one mom, "My kid wouldn't be caught dead with a juice box. But Capri Sun is OK." Back in the cafeteria, some marketers pay to print their advertising on lunchroom menus. The marketer gains a presence in front of children, and the school saves money on the cost of producing the menu.

Play: Kids long for this moment, when the structured part of school gives way to a few moments of independence and choice. Words like handball, kickball, sandbox, and hopscotch are familiar to all. The kids break into groups, boys with boys and girls with girls, friends with friends; they point and laugh and giggle at each other, pass on rumors, and tease the kids who were rebuked by the teacher that morning. It is on the playground where word-of-mouth will make a success or a failure of your brand, be it a packaged item or a movie. Competition breaks out in whatever game is chosen. A hierarchy forms based upon talent at each game. The playground is where characters come alive and reference groups form. And a creative mind can see it all.

And so Matt Groening, creator of "The Simpsons," wrote a book entitled *School Is Hell*. According to Groening, grade-school kids come in 33 varieties, including the Teacher's Pet, the Beauty, Mr. Cool, the Brain, the Dunce, the Copy Cat, the Sissy, the Goof-off, the Bully, the Chatterbox, the Class Clown, the Cry Baby, the Prude, and others. And when they go to high school, they turn into 81 types—such as Super Jock, Prom Queen, the Rich Kid, Cheerleader, King of Snobs, Duchess of Snobs, Brainiac, Surfer, and so on.

Hollywood has used such stereotypes quite a bit. The comedy *Revenge of the Nerds* drew from many of them. The more serious film *The Breakfast Club,* in which high school students of different backgrounds were thrown together in detention, made for a rather fascinating portrayal of teen lives. It all began, however, with a keen observation that someone made about the groups of kids who form associations on the playground.

Afternoon: More studies ensue, perhaps history, art, or music. Perhaps there is a fieldtrip to a museum or zoo, if the students did not already visit it in the morning.

The idea for the "Magic School Bus," in fact, was born from a child's common association with a fieldtrip. Just add an ounce of magic, a dash of transformation, and a fascinating teacher—Ms. Frizzle—and you have it all. This is a school bus that can fly, submerge, shrink, or whatever, in order to take the child on a journey as far as outer space and as close as within the human body, thus helping him learn more about the world. It is amazing that such a simple item as a school bus can become something so grand. It required only that a creative mind observe the common and make it special. The "Magic School Bus" is updated by extending stories across educational subjects and platforms (e.g., books, CD-ROMs, videogames, home videos, toys, etc.). It has become an Ever-Cool.

Going Home: Homework is given out, assignments are explained to the groan of the entire class, then a bell rings and the kids run, not walk, across the school yard. Some kids go to an afterschool care group until working parents can pick them up. Others run off to baseball practice or music lessons.

Marketers have found opportunities here, too. Daycare centers have sprung up across the nation. Afterschool art, music, and sport classes and associations are practically a cottage industry. For those kids who are bound for home, the Kids on the Go taxi service can get them there as well. Broadcasters run programming to reach the child who arrives home from school and wants to watch television before beginning homework.

This structured, daily cycle reoccurs five days a week for twelve years, not counting kindergarten and preschool. For kids, such structure can be confining, controlling, and frustrating—especially if a child's particular teacher does not engage a child's psyche to aid the learning process. Principles and teachers rule, so kids fantasize: what if they, instead, had the control? What if they, instead, ruled? What if they had the guts to ditch school altogether? And so some empathetic, creative mind conceived of the film *Ferris Bueller's Day Off*, featuring a savvy teen who played hooky for a day, managed to fool his parents, and evade a wily principal—thus wrestling control from all those who sought to take it from him. This was a common observation made delightful.

A Marketer's Contribution

There is a far more important side to a marketer's role in education, however. In its May 6, 1996, issue, *Newsweek* reported that IQ scores have risen sharply in the developed world since the beginning of this century. In fact, they have increased some 24 points in the United States, with similar gains in other developed countries. The reason for the increase is under debate. Some suspect that children have higher IQs through nurture, better diet, and exposure to more stimulating environments with museums and zoos. Some suggest IQs are rising simply because kids are more exposed to, and thus familiar with, a plethora of IQ-like brain teasers such as puzzles and mazes that appear in such places as on a McDonald's Happy Meal box. Still, a Yale University study found that watching "Barney & Friends" and then participating in learning activities helps children from low-income and culturally diverse backgrounds better prepare for school.

It seems that marketers may be at least partially responsible in a positive way for educating our youth, all because many of them have been able to make a connection between education and the motivations that live at the core of a child's heart.

There are other interesting consequences of a more educated child, making an impact in ways we do not readily see. "For Jonny Quest," says Rob Maresca, vice-president of marketing at Hanna-Barbera, "nationwide qualitative research indicated that our primary audience [boys 6-11] was tired of spandex-clad superheros and wanted a show that respected their intelligence . . . so we made sure that the blend of characters was balanced, with as much brain as brawn." Such thinking gave "The Real Adventures of Jonny Quest" an initial, successful launch.

Brand Challenges

- Can you make learning engaging by satisfying a child's psyche?
- Can your brand fit into the schoolday, and if so, where?
- Can you create a story that can capture a child's educational and interpersonal struggles and triumphs that occur from 8:30 A.M. to 3:30 P.M. Monday through Friday?

14

Analyze Their Play

It's hard for the modern generation to understand Thoreau, who lived beside a pond but didn't own water skis or a snorkle.
—Bill Vaughan

PLAY IS THE THING. Ask any kid, "So, Johnny, what do you want to do today?"

Chances are he is *not* apt to reply with a sincere smile, "While I could go to baseball practice or to Disneyland, I think I'd much rather study math." Although that is every parent's dream, it is not going to happen in this century (unless far more educators can engage a child's psyche).

This chapter will discuss a child's leisure activities—what I call "play"—the emotions that "play" satisfies, and how the marketer can use such knowledge to create or maintain Ever-Cools.

PLAY: *To exercise or employ oneself in diversion, amusement, or recreation*

The very word *play* can do more for a sour disposition than any medicine or elixir known to either civilized or aboriginal man. Just say that magic word to a group of children and watch as exuberant, anticipating smiles wash over their lips. Here is why:

Play is control and freedom. The whole notion of play, and I use the word to encompass any form of leisure from watching television to playground games to simply hanging

159

Mmmom! Bobby says I have to call him
"most exalted power being of the universe"
for the rest of my life!

out with friends, represents a flight from responsibility forced upon them by others. "I get to do what I want," says one child. And for the most part, that is right. He gets to hang with his friends, to see a movie, to watch television, to play videogames. It is his time; there are few rules and even fewer anxious moments brought on by the rigors of schools, tests, and household duties.

Play is a straight arrow that shoots right into a child's heart, thus filling emotional needs buried within. So as odd as this may sound, kids are not satisfied by the mere act of "watching" television, "playing" videogames, or "reading" a book, per se. That is an observation made by adults from afar. The kid, at the bottom of it all, cares little about such "physical" things, which are simply means to achieve more important ends. A child really cares about the feeling of power he gets when he destroys vile monsters, such as the ones that challenge him in the computer game of DOOM. He cares about his own fantasies he sees fulfilled when he visits Disneyland. She cares about belonging to a company of friends, like the ones in the book series *The Baby-sitters Club*. In this context, a boy can bury himself in the classic tale of overcoming adversity afforded by Robert Louis Stevenson's *Treasure Island* or by playing Sega's Sonic the Hedgehog. She can feel the thrill of finding the criminal from tales of Arthur Conan Doyle's *Sherlock Holmes* or from the intriguing computer game of Myst. This may offend those who prefer the written word, but characters from both the printed page and the technological one can and do stimulate similar, core emotions. They compete head-on for a child's heart. So if kids spend more time with Sonic than Sherlock, it is because the graphics, sound, and "control" they feel from the videogame add mightily to the realism by stimulating multiple senses, which heighten emotional response.

Play is a goal and also a reward in many households. It is a tool some parents use to get the child to perform specified tasks. "You can't go out and play until you finish all your homework," says Dad, again and again. That makes play all the more precious and desired.

Faces of Play

The many faces of play are shown in Exhibit #14-1. This is the broadest expression of play, defined by the task: "Describe a really fun time." The responses given by eight- to twelve-year-old children included sports, visiting theme parks, and just hanging out with friends. The gender differences are readily apparent, with boys focusing more on sports and girls more on friends.

What is most interesting about this list is what is not prominent. Television is not mentioned—and that is fascinating. Kids, it seems, would rather be out and about, engaged in sports and activities, than in the home watching the tube. Could it be that kids, only when asked to come inside the home, resort to the television because their first choice, to be playing outside, has been taken from them? Perhaps that is why sports-related videogames do so well, for they are surrogates for the real thing that the child, for whatever reason, is unable to engage in at that particular moment. In fact, one study reported that weekly television viewing among children ages two to eleven is down significantly versus a decade ago. Videos, videogames, and personal computers are encroaching on standard television viewing. In effect, they compete to satisfy the same emotional needs.

The Winners Circle

Marketers who have succeeded within the many categories of play did so because they found the best way to fulfill those emotional needs, via a sport, videogame, theme park, movie, etc. The 1995 winner's circle (a partial list) can be seen in Exhibit #14-2. Scan down the list of play (and some play-related) categories and ascertain what emotional need each item probably satisfies within the child—is it strength/power, gross/bizarre/silly, beauty, nurturing, mastery/winning,

Exhibit #14-1

<u>Faces of Play</u>

Describe a really fun time...

	Kids Ages 8-12	
	<u>Boys</u>	<u>Girls</u>
Sports/activities	27%	11%
Theme parks	22%	20%
Games/toys	11%	–
Friends	10%	23%
Outdoor adventure	6%	2%
Movies	4%	–
Travel	4%	5%
Summer vacation	3%	–
Parties	3%	5%
The shopping mall	2%	8%
Girls	2%	–
The beach	1%	4%
Christmas/presents	1%	–
Boys	–	8%
Restaurant	–	3%
School	–	2%

Source: 1995 Zandl Report, The Zandl Group

resolving fears, seeking control, achieving a specific fantasy for riches or fame, or gratifying senses or others?

Gatorade is *the* power drink. Nike provides power in an attitude. Mortal Kombat software allows the child to thwart evil. The MONOPOLY board game gives the child an opportunity to fulfill a "get rich" fantasy and beat his friends in the process, if only for an hour or two. Music of Green Day and Boyz II Men touches a wide range of emotions within kids and teens, ranging from rebellion to romance. *Goosebumps* entertains by tickling a child's fears. Bugs Bunny is silly and outrageous and as sophisticated or as slapstick as he wants to be. "Rugrats," a Nickelodeon program, is nurturing and witty all at once. *Sports Illustrated* touches a boy's desire to compete and to win, while *'Teen* magazine affords the girl an opportunity to think of fashion, glamour, and romance.

Some categories hide all the specific emotions that underpin their success. For example, many kids list Disney as a popular vacation destination. There are a multitude of emotions connected with a Disney theme park. While the most prominent among them is fantasy fulfillment (e.g., sliding down the Matterhorn), others include conquering fears (e.g., thrill rides), gratifying the senses (e.g., light and laser shows), and even being nurtured (e.g., in-costume characters).

The list in Exhibit #14-2, in essence, is a floodgate of emotions—not things, objects, or programs. These activities and objects are important devices constructed in a fashion to touch a child's heart and bring a smile into a child's world.

This list also conveys other insights. Favorite actors for boys, for example, include both Jim Carrey, who can exhibit gross, bizarre, or silly behavior; as well as Arnold Schwarzenegger, who embodies strength and power. These two characters are so different in what they convey, each probably never really competes head to head for a child's attention. Instead, each satisfies a different part of a child's psyche. Both can easily cohabitate within the child's mind. It is more likely that Arnold Schwarzenegger competes with

Exhibit #14-2

Winner's Circle

Favorite...	**Boys**	**Girls**
	Kids Ages 8-12	
Sports beverage	Gatorade	Gatorade
Shoes	Nike	Nike
Jeans	Levi	Levi
Vacation	Florida	Florida
	Disney	Disney
Restaurant	McDonald's	McDonald's
Video/computer game	Mortal Kombat	Nintendo
Board game	Monopoly	Monopoly
Music	Green Day	Boyz II Men
TV shows	Simpsons	Full House
	Power Rangers	Home Improvement
	Home Improvement	Friends
Actor	Jim Carrey	Jim Carrey
	Jean-Claude Van Damme	Jonathan Taylor Thomas
	Arnold Schwarzenegger	Brad Pitt
Comic/cartoon	X-men	Garfield
	Spiderman	Rugrats
	Bugs Bunny	Bugs Bunny
Movie	Dumb and Dumber	Lion King
	The Mask	The Mask
Book (recent)	Goosebumps	Goosebumps
	–	Baby-Sitters Club
Magazine	Sports Illustrated	Teen

Source: 1995 Zandl Report–Partial list, The Zandl Group

Jean-Claude Van Damme. So as every studio executive knows, it is not wise to have two action adventures fall on the same opening weekend—but a comedy and a thriller, maybe.

Ever-Cools

Also notice that many items on the list have been in the public eye for years, suggesting that in one fashion or another they cracked the Ever-Cool formula. The Nike brand helps stay fresh with a stream of celebrity endorse-ments. McDonald's stays current with its ever-changing pro-motions, as well as with the broader role it plays in a child's life. *Goosebumps* stays fresh with each book. Disney stays fresh with each successful film it introduces, which spills over into the theme parks by way of an attraction or a parade born out of the film itself. All, of course, contempo-rize many other elements of their marketing mix; but for most, there is one element that carries a disproportional burden for contemporizing the brand.

Games such as MONOPOLY are interesting cases, as cited earlier. They are purchased by each generation, but they change little over the years. The MONOPOLY board game so precisely targets our desire to be rich that no com-petitor can unseat it.

THE FAD: *A temporary fashion, manner of conduct, etc., especially one followed enthusiastically by a group*

Some play items do not have staying power and are even-tually deemed a fad. They make the "what's cool" list for a season, or even a couple years, and then they are gone. In five years, it will be interesting to see if Exhibit #14-2 still con-tains names like Power Rangers, Mortal Kombat, X-Men, and Brad Pitt. Are they fads or Ever-Cools? Only time will tell.

Fads die because they do not successfully evolve with chil-dren. This can be because the creator or marketer does not have the creativity to keep it fresh. Or, the idea, itself, was too narrow in scope to begin with and too limited in terms of how it could be made fresh again.

The fad, however, is a great vehicle to use to make an existing brand look contemporary. Pogs was one of these. The game began at Hawaii's Haleakala Dairy decades ago and was played with the round cardboard caps of glass milk and juice bottles. Kids would stack the caps high, then hit the top of the stack with a heavy rounded "slammer" to see how many "pogs" they could turn over as the pile fell to the floor. Those that turn over belonged to the child who "slammed" them. Then it is the next child's turn. Marketers noted Pogs' growing popularity for both playing and collecting and then fueled the craze by offering Pogs in many colorful designs and interesting packaging containers, as well as a multitude of promotional offers and a heavy barrage of media weight. These efforts extended the longevity of Pogs for a time. As I write this, however, the fad is dying, doomed by its inability to continuously re-invent itself. It was a fad other marketers used to make their own brands look cool via promotions. It was not a long-term brand itself.

Fads can come from anywhere, particularly from those categories that are perishable in nature such as toys, films, and programming. But if there is one category that is the birthplace of many fads, it is in the performing arts. Music, as noted earlier, has an interesting role in the birth of fads. Popular music becomes such because it pulls at a child's emotional heartstrings. For tweens and teens, those heartstrings might include romance, rebellion, independence, and angst. When kids like the music, they begin to inspect the artist who performs it. The kids note the performer's style of clothes, manner of speech, dance, and attitude and begin to relate to the same. Suddenly, not only does a certain performing artist make the charts, but specific fashions, language, and attitude break onto the scene as well. The fashion known as the "grunge" look, for example, was comprised of down-to-earth flannel shirts, combat boots, and ripped jeans. It was popularized by the group Nirvana, a band out of Seattle that featured Kurt Cobain. Rap music, created in cities across the nation by African-Americans, led to baggy urban street fashions. For the baby boomers among you, remember that Olympic medalist Dorothy Hamill popularized a short, sassy hair fashion that became known as the "wedge."

A Marketer's Use of Play

Marketers can use the knowledge of a child's play activities and current interests in several ways. First, they can

review "what's cool" and "what's not" in lists such as that in
Exhibit #14-2 in hopes of discovering the emotional need
not currently being fulfilled. I call these "Psyche Gaps,"
places within a child's psyche that are not being satisfied.
That is where opportunities exist for potentially new brands
and ideas. In 1995, for example, where was the film that targeted a boy's desire to save the world? Where was the girl's
version of *Big*, a film where a girl obtains her desire to be
older? Where was the computer game that allowed a boy to
feel or perhaps have a chance to truly *be* famous? Where
was the theme park devoted to nothing but the gross and
the bizarre, with a veritable slime pit at the bottom of every
roller coaster? Or where was the *Goosebumps* theme park,
devoted solely to scaring customers out of their wits via
haunted attractions? Where was the themed restaurant that
touched a child's nature to be gross, or the one that puts
him in control of the food's preparation? These were either
bad ideas, lost opportunities, or simply ones not executed
well enough or broadly enough to have been a mega-hit.
The process of searching for psyche gaps is invaluable, for
it can help the marketer create a new brand idea; chapter
16 will show you how.

Marketers keep their existing brands Ever-Cool by associating them with those play activities children participate in.
This might include grass-roots marketing via sponsorships
of Little League teams, to sponsorship of the Olympics, to
having venues at popular theme parks. A common
approach is to routinely buy licenses that reflect a popular
play icon, like Hercules.

Marketers can also be inventive by creating marketing
ideas that reflect a kid's play culture. A great example is
Amurol Confections, another winner of the Ever-Cool award.
Amurol Confections competes in the gum and candy markets. Among other things, they created containers for their
products that reflect contemporary kid's culture. Containers
have taken on the appearance of beepers, checkbooks, pad-

locks, and calculators. They have also included Nickelodeon-branded items as well. Hence, Amurol Confections delivers a great, flavorful gum dressed up in a current fad or trend. And they have been quite successful doing so.

Another Ever-Cool winner is Kraft Macaroni & Cheese Dinner. Once shaped like a small noodle, the macaroni is now shaped like contemporary icons reflecting a kid's world. As I open my own kitchen pantry, I see Kraft Macaroni & Cheese dinners with themes and noodles shaped like popular TV programs (e.g., "Animaniacs"), classic characters (e.g., "The Flintstones"), and even the ABCs. The great taste stays timeless, the shape changes to reflect, in a large part, many of the child's favorite leisure activities. If you laid end-to-end all of the boxes of Kraft Marcaroni & Cheese sold annually in the United States, they would stretch from New York to Los Angeles and back again more than nine times.

The various play activities cited throughout this chapter are the marketers' playthings. They are conduits to satisfying a kid's heart. If a marketer decides, for example, to target a boy's need for strength and power, she can do so at the movies, in the playground, in a book, in a recording, in a breakfast cereal, and in a dozen other places and items. The ideas are limitless.

Brand Challenges

- Is your brand in the winner's circle—is it the best in fulfilling a child's emotional needs? If so, which needs does it fulfill?

- Have you identified those emotional needs—psyche gaps—which have not been satisfied in your category? Do these gaps represent potential new brands or ideas?

- Is your existing brand kept Ever-Cool by associating itself with a broad range of kids' play activities?

**Don't worry, Mom. We'll put your drapes back
when we're done playing.**

15

Live in Their Special World

For every man the world is as fresh as it was at the first day,
and as full of untold novelties for him who has the eyes to see them.
—Thomas Henry Huxley (1825-1895)

A BUSINESSMAN MAY BE SITTING AT A RESTAURANT, engaged in a business lunch, when a waitress approaches wearing a familiar perfume. Suddenly, his memory may be catapulted back thirty years, perhaps to a sixth-grade classroom where an English teacher wore the same fragrance. Images may fill the businessman's mind, of where he sat in that classroom, of the maps that adorned the walls, of vague recollections of kids' faces about him, their names too distant in time to remember. He might feel joy or sorrow in those images, depending on his particular experiences in that class so long ago. Either a comforting smile or a heartfelt wince may then briefly come to his expression even as he pretends to listen to his associate discuss quarterly results. And it all transpires in a few precious seconds of time. It is almost supernatural in the way a physical object can—on just sight, smell, touch, or hearing—impact us.

TALISMAN: *An object marked with magical signs and believed to confer on its bearer supernatural powers or protection*

So objects—tangible and otherwise—are triggers to recollections and emotions. And these associations begin to

171

form very early on when things and feelings meet within a child's mind, commingle, and become forever linked. Objects of childhood, then, can be very powerful, emotional lightning rods, indeed.

This chapter is about some of the objects of childhood that can give way to an array of feelings, some of which may carry into adulthood. I cannot possibly list all the objects in a child's world that ignite emotions. This chapter serves only to raise your awareness that while adults may consider something to be common, for kids it can be special. So take nothing for granted. First I will review an assorted list of talismans (i.e., special icons, places, events, things, and themes) and their associated emotions. Then, I will discuss how some marketers have used each to help build both their new and existing brands.

Special Icons

Wishes are special, not only because of the hope a child feels when making a wish, but because the wish just might come true. It is the exciting anticipation, pure and simple. Wishes are the heart's desires that reach a child's consciousness, if not his lips. They are precious and treated as such by children.

Kisses and **hugs** express love and comfort for the child. They demonstrate sharing, warmth, and belonging. These very powerful feelings can be expressed with the mere touch of another human being. A squeeze can yield a tender moment.

Teardrops are the physical manifestation of the human heart and the psyche. A tear is a special talisman to the child, for it denotes the expression held within that is suddenly apparent for all to see. As children grow older, they hide their tears, avoid the parental squeeze, and suppress emotion. But the tear, the warmth, and the desire to be hugged is there, waiting to be expressed.

Secrets are empowering. If I know a secret, I not only

feel special, but I have an invisible control over others who do not know the secret. "I have a secret and I can't tell you," is the most powerful phrase on the playground. It ensures that those who utter such a sentence will be surrounded and followed until the secret is revealed—instant popularity.

Magic is empowering. The word connotes powers and supernatural abilities that defy the physical world. Magic can be good or evil and gives its user the power to control and amaze others.

Special Places

The word *home* conjures up many emotions: safety, comfort, belonging, retreat—a haven from the rest of the world. A home is a child's most precious possession, for it is the center of his world and his existence.

The **bedroom** is the child's innermost sanctuary where she feels comfort and safety against an uncontrollable world. Here a child obtains a sense of control. "This is my room," a child will say, and the implied, "so I can do with it as I wish" is ever-present. Bedrooms are also places where a child feels he can express himself with art, trophies, posters, you name it. There is pride in that. It is also a place where fantasy reins. Every mother has probably experienced the situation of approaching her child's room only to hear her daughter talking to her doll or her son pretending he's in a spaceship and not in a bedroom at all. A bedroom is a time and place fantasy machine. As such, it is a place of wonder, a harbor from reality.

Attics and **basements** are places of demons, waiting to swallow a child whole, or so some kids may think. They are dark places where children are often told not to go, which heightens both a child's curiosity and his fear. They are places to be avoided, yet at the same time, conquered.

Tree houses and **forts** inspire independence, much the same as a bedroom does. But they are also places to be defended against all interlopers, which makes them places of power and strength, as well of peer approval and acceptance. Club Members Only is a sign first mounted at the entrance of a tree house long before its members will even know adult versions of the same.

Disneyland is a legendary place, the original gold standard of amusement parks. The very name Disney conjures up thoughts of fanciful stories and characters. There is a childlike wonder in that for younger kids. It is also a place to take a date when you get older, where couples go to share thrills and fantasies. The same goes for Walt Disney World.

Roller coaster parks are places to go and test your nerve against giant, demon coasters; to overcome fears; to feel the excitement and pride of spending $20 to win a $5 stuffed animal; and to hang out and bond with friends. And since there are so many tweens and teens present, they are also places where older kids can gawk at members of the opposite sex with relative impunity.

Zoos and **animal parks** tickle a child's curiosity, love of nature, and imagination of what the world might look like beyond the confines of his own neighborhood. Adults will stroll through such a park and take for granted the animals that they have seen a thousand times. But to a child, the variety of wildlife is new, foreign, and intriguing. The gorilla, the tiger, the lion, the zebra, and the snake—they are all truly amazing.

Sports stadiums conjure up aspirations and feelings of power and success. They really are a field of dreams. There is not a kid alive who has attended a football game, gymnastic meet, or ice-skating competition and not thought for a moment, "That could be me!"

Malls are a marketplace of emotional outlets and adventures. And in that marketplace, the child is exposed to many emotions all in one afternoon. The pet shop may bring out feelings of nurturing with its puppies or fears with its tarantulas. The toy store turns a child's head to glamour with Barbie dolls, the idea of good vanquishing evil with G.I. Joe figures, or mastery with arts and crafts. A trip into the music store may touch that part of a child that desires to be seen as older, more independent, or even rebellious depending upon his music selection. As a child gets older, the mall becomes a place to see and be seen by your friends or a potential girl- or boyfriend. As such, malls across America are not just convenient shopping places where you run in and pick up a few needed items—not to a kid, at least. To the child, the mall is a place where many deep-rooted emotional needs get satisfied, all at once.

Toy, candy, and **ice-cream stores** are places where your desires could be fulfilled, if only money grew on trees. There is a carnival atmosphere here, touching off an array of emotions that spans from great anticipation to intense joy for those kids lucky enough to get something and to the feelings of discouragement and want for those who do not.

Special Events

Christmas and **Hanukkah** are the pivotal days on most kids' calendars. All other dates revolve around them. Presents, sweets, stories, and celebrations each produce excitement within the child, even as the parent attempts to ensure that the child understands the spiritual significance of the holidays. So a child experiences anticipation, joy, hope, thrills, and understanding.

Birthdays allow the child to feel older, more mature. For there is a pecking order in the child's kingdom. Age, perhaps more than any other factor, gives a child authority over those younger. That is why if a mother tells a neighbor that her child is five, her nearby child will correct her with, "I'm 5½." The "half" matters. A growing child feels pride, empowerment, and accomplishment. And of course, there is the joy of presents!

Halloween allows a child to role play, while getting his hands on as much candy as is humanly possible. Many emotions abound on this day. Children can live their aspirations by dressing up as their heroes. They can turn their fears into glory by donning the likeness of hideous monsters and using that role to make others fear them. That is empowerment to a child. Most adults cannot see past the costumes and the candy, but Halloween fulfills fantasies, as well as the sweet tooth.

Achieving a "first" has special emotions. The first day of school can produce both fear of social acceptance and the joy of re-bonding with former friends. The first day of summer vacation makes a child feel free, unrestrained, and rebellious. The first kiss from a classmate can give rise to feelings from joy and maturity to those of dread and nausea. The first sleep-over can make a child feel more mature and more independent while strengthening the bonds with friends.

Special Things

Receiving **mail** is important for a child, for it makes him feel special and older. It says that someone considered the child important enough to send him something. It means that the child has, indeed, an identity. Plus, there is the added, excited anticipation of seeing what items the mail has brought.

Parties and **presents** are pure joy—the more, the bigger, the better. To get a present that all other kids covet is better still. To be the first in your neighborhood to get it is the best. This brings pride, self-importance, and accomplishment. And of course, there is the specific emotion that each present might deliver.

Maps are special pieces of paper that describe the immense, physical world. They reveal knowledge, which makes a child treat them with awe. And if such a map leads to a buried treasure, then they are coveted; the child who possesses such a document feels powerful.

Books are gateways to stories of grand and fanciful worlds that the child can visit within the confines and security of his own home. And those books, just as videogames and computer games, allow him to play the role of some central character, perhaps one whose perseverance saves a medieval castle from some evil dragon. Fear, bravery, and triumph are but a few emotions found within the pages of a good story.

Report cards are either sources of joy, accomplishment, and pride, or a source of fret and feelings of inadequacy. The same can be said for tests.

Special Themes

There are special, recurring themes that children forever love, for they embrace feelings of excitement, comfort, or awe. These include animal themes that span from insects to sea creatures, birds, horses, dogs, cats, dinosaurs, and more. Special themes also includes historical icons from Ancient Greek heroes to Vikings, biblical tales of David and Goliath, and stories about King Arthur, wizards, cowboys, and the Wild West. The "unknown" has always peeked a child's inquisitive nature as well and has included such questions as: what is in the center of the earth? Do space aliens really exist? What is on the ocean floor? Is there a real Loch Ness Monster? Is there a heaven, and what is it like? How does the human body work? What is a rainbow? All of these themes are murals for the creative mind to paint upon—to weave a story, build a toy, or create a promotion that will appeal to a child's heart.

Implications

A child's emotional world is multifaceted, filled with an amazing array of special icons, places, events, things, and themes, all of which elicit an emotional response. A marketer can use his knowledge of such to create a new brand or idea, to contemporize an existing one, or to give a brand greater emotional depth. Here is a sampling.

As noted earlier, Disney uses mightily the concepts of magic, fantasy, and wishes. Cinderella has her fairy godmother. Aladdin has his genie. Dumbo has his magic feather. Wish upon a star and it just might come true—with Disney. Magic, fantasy, and wishes are a very important part of the Disney aura, its brand persona, and its point of difference.

Sea World brings a child face to face with the creatures of the deep. Knott's Berry Farm transports children to the Old West. The above elements are important "parts" of what each brand is, each based upon a theme that kids, young and old, respond to emotionally. The Mall of America in Minnesota targeted an added emotion when it installed a roller coaster ride inside the mall itself. It was not steel and bolts the mall erected, but thrills.

Arkady Leokum enticed a child's natural curiosity when he wrote a book entitled *The Big Book of Tell Me Why*. The book answers hundreds of questions children love to ask such as, "How big is the universe?" and "How do earthworms eat? Nickelodeon's program "Are You Afraid of the Dark?" confronts a child's curious fears of magic and monsters and things that go bump in a kid's attic.

The film *Angels in the Outfield* not only tickled a child's fascination with the afterlife, but it did so in a ballpark, yet another kid interest. The story of *Dr. Doolittle* stretched a child's imagination with strange and wondrous animals. The setting for *Willy Wonka* was in a chocolate factory. *The Nightmare Before Christmas* was a Halloween tale at Christmastime. The film *Toy Story* brought a kid's most valued possessions to life. Alice of Wonderland fame went to a tea party. The hero of the saga, *The Neverending Story*, became part of the book he was reading. Hershey Foods markets the treats of Kisses and Hugs milk chocolate. All of these examples rest upon an icon that, from the beginning, is emotionally laden.

Some marketers mail magazines to the child because they know it strengthens the emotional bond. Marketers add the word *magic* to any brand that might have a "revealing" or transformation feature (e.g., *Magic School Bus*) because they know kids respond to the word emotionally. They add the word *secret* when features are hidden and just waiting to be revealed to the amazement of those watching. Both *magic* and *secret* are talisman words, and they are Ever-Cool. Marketers have also recognized the importance of a child's bedroom. Some have developed posters to be hung there and bedsheets to be spread, while others have found ways to protect it from intruders.

Interestingly, while many things within a kid's world have emotional content, they can be treated emotionless until the creative mind imbues it in a fashion to touch a designated part of a child's heart. In an earlier chapter, I cited that a ghost can be made either nurturing, as in *Casper,* or menacing, as in *Ghostbusters.* Similarly, we can take a dinosaur, fatten him up, paint him purple, and have him sing kid songs in order to nurture and to teach preschoolers. So Barney was born. Or we can take a dinosaur, make it real, make it terrifying, turn it loose on an island, and let nature take its course—a seed of an idea for *Jurassic Park,* a place where kids struggle for survival, and yet triumph over the beasts in the end. The icon of the dinosaur is the same in either case, but the way it is handled produces two quite different brands, and two quite different emotional reponses.

This is all to say that children hold many things dear. They attach to them special meaning and special emotions. Knowing this, a marketer can better create and connect his brand to the child in a richer, deeper way by tapping into the many talismans that already exist. But it is one thing to cite examples of what others have done. It is far more difficult to generate successful ideas yourself. That is the focus of Part IV.

Brand Challenges

- How can your brand immerse itself in a kid's special world? How can it tap into one, or many, of the talismans that already exist? Can your brand weave itself into a child's
    - Special icons?
    - Special places?
    - Special events?
    - Special things?
    - Special themes?

PART IV
Marketing to a Child's Heart

Marketing to a Child's Heart

All the knowledge conveyed thus far is worthless unless the marketer can use it to create brands, build brands, and keep them Ever-Cool.

This section is about marketing to a child's heart. It begins by providing tools that will help the marketer generate a flow of ideas for new brands (chapter 16). It then discusses how those brands can be brought to life in effective advertising (chapter 17). But long-term success will be enhanced if the marketer has a flow of the right information at the right time, which will be reviewed in the chapter on research (chapter 18). And because marketing to kids can be rather controversial, the topic of marketing standards and ethics will be reviewed as well (chapter 19). Finally, the book will conclude with some observations about prominent kid brands and their lifelong relationship with the child (chapter 20).

16

Develop Kid-Appealing Products

All achievement, all earned riches,
have their beginning in an idea!
—Napoleon Hill
Author of *Think and Grow Rich*

IN ONE ANALYSIS CONDUCTED across hundreds of kid-product launches, it was found, as one might expect, that a primary determinant of a product's success is its innate appeal. It is nice to have your judgment validated.

Successful marketing plans begin with a product or service that kids love. And that success cannot begin until somebody, somewhere, has an idea worth loving. But good ideas are hard to come by, which is why many marketers employ departments of creative thinkers, whether they be toy designers, food developers, writers, artists, or whoever. And still, many of them are not trained to generate a consistent flow of ideas. Instead, ideas are born haphazardly while creative people are in the shower, taking a walk, at the supermarket, or in casual brainstorming sessions with colleagues.

Connect the Unconnected

A few creative men and women have an innate ability to generate a huge volume of ideas, and they are continually shaking the creative tree. Such special minds have an

I must say, this résumé is very impressive.

uncanny ability to see relationships between trends, events, or things that few others can readily see, and in that vision they find a plethora of ideas. To quote William Plomer:

> It is the function of creative men [and women] to perceive the relations between thoughts, or things, or forms of expression that may seem utterly different, and to be able to combine them into some new forms—the power to connect the seemingly unconnected.

You have all seen some variation of this commercial: Two strangers are walking toward each other, each eating a different treat, when they inadvertently bump and mesh the treats together. "You've got your peanut butter in my chocolate," says the first. "You've got your chocolate in my peanut butter," corrects the second. And so, Reese's Peanut Butter Cups were born. This connection of the "seemingly unconnected" has a rather long history. It was John Montagu (1718-1792) who first placed meat between two slices of bread. That seems simple enough, but until that time, civilization could not find any other relationship between the two foods other than to eat the bread and the meat in separate mouthfuls. Montagu, whose official title was the fourth earl of Sandwich, ate his meat and bread in this convenient, handy combination so he would not have to leave the gambling table to eat a formal, proper meal. Necessity caused him to see a relationship others had missed.

Forcing Relationships: Matrixing

By forcing our eyes to see relationships, we help our brain consider the ideas that are born from them. This can be accomplished with a system I call *matrixing*, a simple process of putting various categories of items in front of our eyes, side by side, in a fashion that will help us to easily mix and match them. The items we will force together are those that we have discussed throughout this book.

The emphasis will be upon developing ideas for new brands that, by design, contain emotional benefits that satisfy a child's heart. By way of examples, I will demonstrate how matrixing works across very diverse categories. The basics are similar, so you can easily add your own industry and categories to the matrices provided.

One very simple matrix is in Exhibit #16-1. The first column simply lists different categories a marketer may be targeting (e.g., sports/activities, toys, snacks, restaurants, bedding, theme parks, etc.). The second column contains key elements of a kid's emotional psyche. This ensures that when we develop ideas, we do so with a child's heart in mind. The third column reminds us to gratify the child's senses, thus challenging us to find a feature that helps us satisfy the psyche in a way that distinguishes our new brand from competitive offerings. The fourth column will help us generate ideas within the context of a kid's world and culture: from trends and fads to family and a child's timeless interests. The fifth column lists the marketing options at our disposal to keep the new brand fresh year after year—Ever-Cool. We might, for example, develop an idea where the product is re-invented each year (e.g., Barbie dolls); we might instead develop one in which we simply change the shape of the product (e.g., Kraft Macaroni & Cheese dinners); we might change the outer container or packaging (e.g., PEZ Candy or Amurol Confections); we might add contemporary variety (e.g., Baskin-Robbins or Crayola crayons); or we might develop one in which we alter the promotional tie-in (e.g., McDonald's Happy Meal). Of course, we can use all of the above, but most brands lead with one avenue and supplement with the others. In any case, the advertising can be contemporized regardless.

I have used such matrices to help creative minds generate all types of ideas. It helps structure their thinking while giving them the right fodder for idea generation. The most promising ideas are those that satisfy a key emotion that no

Exhibit #16-1
Kids' Idea Matrix

#1 PRODUCT CATEGORY	#2 KID PSYCHE	#3 KEY FEATURES/SENSORY	#4 KIDS' WORLD/CULTURE			#5 MKT OPTIONS
Sports/Activities	Win/Master	Sight	**World Awareness**	**Family Life**	**School**	**Marketing Options**
Bikes	Control/Empowerment	Sound	Environment	Parents	Leaning	Product/Variety
Skateboards			World Peace	Grandparents	Teachers	Packaging
Equipment (e.g. Balls)	Love/Affection	Smell	Diversity	Brothers/Sisters	Homework	Promotion
etc			Crime	Greater Independence	Field Trips	Advertising
Toys	Independence/Rebellious	Taste	etc	etc	Lunch Boxes	etc
Male Action			**Interests**	**Animals**	**Sports**	
Games	Outrageous/Silly	Touch	Music/Movies	Dogs	Soccer	
Yo-Yo			TV/Computers	Cats	Basketball	
etc	Bravery/Fears	Activate	Toys/Games	Horses	Swimming	
Snacks			Books	Fish	Baseball/Softball	
Cookies	Girls	Transform	etc	Turtles	Skating	
Chips	Beauty/Glamour			etc	etc	
etc	Nurturing	Form/Shapes	**Special Themes**	**Special Things/Icons**	**Special Places**	
Restaurants		Clusters	Vikings/Wizards	Wishes	Bedrooms	
Pizza	Boys	Balls/Puffs/Bars	Cavemen/Dinosaurs	Kisses & Hugs	Attics/Basements	
Burger	Strength/Power	Squares/Triangles	Ghosts	Secrets	The Mall	
etc	Good vs. Evil	Twists/Filled	UFO's/Space	Magic	Tree Houses	
Bedding	Gross/Bizarre	etc	Rainbows	Parties	Zoos/Theme Parks	
Pillows			etc	Maps	etc	
Sheets		**Flavors**		etc		
etc		Chocolate/Vanilla				
Theme Parks		Strawberry				
etc		etc				
Etc						

current competitor has claimed, thus filling the psyche gaps described earlier. That is the ultimate goal.

Matrixing in Action

Examples of how to use this matrix to generate ideas are below. In total, all the ideas presented in this chapter took less than thirty minutes to develop, so some ideas may appear more interesting than others. Some will be more unique. Some may already be in existence in one form or another; I just may be unaware. The ideas are presented only to demonstrate how the matrix works. I have also included fictitious brand names for each idea. To use this matrix, we simply move from left to right, mixing and matching as we go, or just bounce around each column until we catch a glimpse of a relationship. Here we go:

- Let's say you make sports/activity related products (column #1). In fact, you make bikes. Moving to column #2, we can decide that this bike idea will touch a boy's desire for strength and power (that portion of his psyche). If this bike makes the boy feel powerful, it should be powerful itself. If so, perhaps the bike can make battle sounds in order to gratify a boy's senses (sensory, column #3). It could even look like a jet fighter. Perhaps it even contains a water cannon that the boy can activate with a push of his thumb on the bike's handle, to squirt a stream of water to thwart evil. We will call it BattleBike. Suddenly, we can envision seven- and eight-year-old boys zooming about as though they were in a jet fighter at 20,000 feet and climbing while they squirt make-believe villains everywhere. But how do we contemporize our bike year after year (column #5)? We could buy the license to whatever "power" icon is popular, such as Mighty Morphin Power Rangers one year and something else the next. Then we fashion the bike's decals, colors, etc., accordingly. Or we invent our own power icons, a line of superheroes and their superbikes.

- Jumping back to column #1, we can change our minds and decide it is not a bike at all, but a skateboard idea. With just a press of our toe on a button of our BattleBoard, a stream of water shoots some ten yards. That would certainly be different than current skateboards. Different parts of a boy's psyche are satisfied. Different sensory elements are targeted. Both the bike and skateboard ideas would probably appeal more to boys of the gender-focused and tween stages.

- If you think this concept is too violent, we can create a line of sports balls (e.g., softballs and basketballs) that emotionally rewards a child when he plays with the ball. Via a voice chip embedded in the ball, the child is congratulated (e.g., "Way to go!") whenever he makes a basket with the basketball or catches the softball successfully. We can call it BallStars. To keep it current, we can change the voice's statement each year or use whatever celebrity voices are popular, as well as introduce new sports each year (e.g., soccer, handball, etc.).

- Or we can dip into toys this time by taking a yo-yo and making it gross to appeal to a boy's psyche. It could make various bodily sounds, to appeal to a boy's senses, every time it rises or falls. We could call it Yo-Gross. We can keep it current each year by licensing a gross sound from a "gross" character who is popular that year (e.g., "Ren & Stimpy," Jim Carrey, etc.).

- Let us say you are a snack manufacturer. We can create a cookie that transforms from a powdery brown to all the colors of the rainbow (part of a kid's world) when dipped in milk, to appeal to the senses. We can also include a treasure in every box for the child to discover, to satisfy the child's need to win. And why not, for there is always a treasure at the end of a rainbow! We will call it RainBOWS. We can keep it contemporary by continuously selecting promotional premiums that are "treasure" related, thus tying into the treasure the child will find at the end of the rainbow. We could also use the "reveal" feature to include secret messages on certain cookies to tie into sweepstakes and promotions.

- Or we could make snack chips that have two varieties, one specially designed with the vitamins needed to help a boy's body grow strong so he can better compete and win, the other fortified with the right combination of vitamins to help a girl do the same. We can call them PowerChips for Boys and PowerChips for Girls. Perhaps the advertising campaign can depict boys and girls competing against each other in tests of strength, speed, agility, and intelligence—each competitor is powered by a snack chip that best meets his or her specific gender needs. We can keep our new brand current by routinely selecting real-life, but unknown boy and girl champions to grace the package. Perhaps we can even find these champions by conducting our own "champion contests and events" each year in small towns everywhere across the country to pick the boys and girls who best meet our champion standards. That is fame!

- Let us forget corporate life and open up our own pizza restaurant instead. Our special pizzas will not be a boring round. Instead, they will come in various shapes (column #3) that will draw from across a kid's entire world. Such shapes might include hearts to reveal love and affection and to show that you care enough to order the very best; monsters to address the fears—a child can eat the monster of his nightmares; an endangered species to address concerns a child might have. Money could be donated to help the animal whose likeness the child ordered.

We could call them Shazpas. They are pizzas in shapes, for kids who do not just order a pizza, but want it to reflect how they are feeling at the time. Is this a new brand in itself? Perhaps, perhaps not, but it could be an interesting way for, say Pizza Hut, to stay contemporary and Ever-Cool. Shapes can include popular characters and even presidential candidates, to remain current. During a presidential election, for example, customers can "vote" for the candidate of their choice by ordering a pizza shaped in their preferred candidate's likeness. Imagine the continuous PR value.

- But then again, maybe we manufacture kids' bedding (column #1) and are bored with the same old stuff. We want something special for the parent-focused kid who needs security, love, and something to chase fears away. So we make a pillow that plays a recorded lullaby in his mother's own voice every time the child squeezes the pillow. We will call it Lullaby Mom. We can attempt to update it each year by licensing comforting icons to adorn the pillow. We might even figure out a way to put Mom's own face on the pillow, so the child can hug Mom and listen to her lullaby all night long.

- Or we can develop a theme park (column #1) devoted to sports, make that *extreme* sports, where the child is allowed to test his bravery by participating in all kinds of daring activities such as bungee-jumping, parasailing, scuba diving, etc., as well as participate against other kids in sports challenges. We can call the place ParkXtreme. I can hear the advertising challenge: Do you have the nerve to go? Do you have the stamina to succeed? Can you conquer ParkXtreme? We can keep it current each year by introducing more and more extreme games.

Matrix Extensions

Matrices can be configured in a wide variety of ways, depending on the nature of the specific category and upon the elements at the creator's disposal. For some categories we can add a column to the matrix of various technologies in an attempt to add greater sensory gratification. These might include fiber optics, heat-sensitive color change, remote control, food-processing techniques, and others. We can also add a column of other kid brands to help generate ideas for co-branding. Other matrices might include a listing of popular adult brands to help us generate ideas for those adult brands that might be able to translate into a kid's world. And if there is a specific child audience in mind, such as parent-focused kids, we would add a column of all their specific needs to allow the matrix to be driven by a given audience segment.

With the right matrix and just the right mix of elements, a brainstorming session can be quite productive. In one all-day brainstorming session of food products, a team of some twenty creative minds generated more than 100 ideas using just one matrix. In subsequent concept research, several of the ideas hit pay dirt and went on to product development.

Generating Story Ideas

The most intriguing matrices are used for the creation of story ideas, which may become the tender seed of a novel, a screenplay, an episode for a television series, or your own child's next bedtime story. We first begin by understanding what an "idea" is from a storymaker's point of view. For that, I borrow from the book *Writing Screenplays That Sell* by writer and producer Michael Hauge. "Any story idea," says Hauge, "can be expressed in a single sentence: it is a story about a (<u>character</u>) who (<u>action</u>)." Simply, stories are about a character who does or wants something. That something reflects a visible, burning motivation. *Home Alone,* for example, is a story about a boy left by himself who discovers he must defend his home from burglars.

A matrix designed to help generate story ideas is in Exhibit #16-2. Column #1 is the potential character and family circumstance (i.e., life cycle), starting from a child within the womb to someone after death (spirits). Column #2 is a partial list of motivations or needs based on some

Exhibit #16-2

Kids' Story Idea Matrix

#1 LIFE CYCE	#2 FANTASIES	#3 FULFILLMENT	#4 GENRE
Womb	Dumb to Smart	Achievement	Comedy
	Ugly to Pretty	Luck	Action Adventure
Child	Rags to Riches	Magic	Drama
Girl	Weak to Strong	Science	Family
Boy	Novice to Master		Science Fiction
	Underdog to Victor		Crime/Mystery
Young Adult	Injustice to Justice		Horror
College	Helpless to Survivor		Romance
Workforce	Helpless to Saving World		Musical
	Cowardice to Bravery		Western
Maturing Adult	Alone to Companionship		Documentary
Single	Unpopular to Popular (Fame)		Any Combination
Married	Jobless to Employed		
Married w/kids	Employee to Boss		
Single parent	Young to Old to Young		
Other	Small to Big to Small		
	Human to Animal		
Maturing Family	Imaginary to Real		
Kids in College	Inaminate to Alive		
Empty Nesters	Past to Present to Future		
Grandparents	Here to There		
Retired	Visible to Invisible		
Widowed	Dreams to Reality		
	Ground to Flight		
Death	Sick to Well		
	Mortal to Immortal		
	Dead to Alive		
	Hell to Heaven		

common core fantasies such as becoming smart, pretty, rich, strong, and so on. It also contains some rather far-out fantasies such as becoming an animal or trying to get to heaven if you inadvertently ended up in hell. These first two columns gives us a sample character as well as some potential burning motivations. The third column tells us how he or she might fulfill the need, whether it be through achievement, luck, magic, or science—the transformation options discussed in chapter 7 regarding fantasies. The final column gives us our genre options and each is used either alone or in combinations.

In fact, we can immediately find existing films in the matrix. A girl (column #1) who goes from rags to needed riches (column #2) by way of magic (column #3) in a splendid family/musical (column #4) is, of course, Disney's *Cinderella*. Whereas a boy (column #1) who goes from weak to strong (column #2) via achievement born of training (column # 3) in a drama (column #4) sounds like the humble beginnings of the film *The Karate Kid*. On the other hand, if a handful of kids end up transformed from big to small, microscopic in fact, through science, and then go on a hair-raising adventure through their own backyard in an effort to get home, you will have the makings of *Honey, I Shrunk the Kids,* a delightful 1989 film from Walt Disney Productions.

Execution, of course, is 95 percent of the battle in developing a brilliant end product, but the matrix can help the storyteller generate ideas and focus his thoughts before deciding upon which idea he or she wishes to pursue. This is a bare-bones matrix for something as complicated as a story idea and there are far more characters and motivations that can be added to the matrix, but this one is a fun place to start. Once again, I will provide examples of ideas that were generated off this matrix only to demonstrate how the matrix works.

We will begin by picking an item or two from each

column, then let our minds weave a story, giving it context and color. For example, let us create a story about a ten-year-old girl (column #1) who wants desperately to be older (column #2)—say a teen-ager—so she can attract some teen-age boy. We will give our character her wish through science (column #3). But how do we do that? We add context. Perhaps the Tinkerbell lip gloss she was recently given by her parents ("Too babyish," she thinks) was inadvertently contaminated at the factory with an experimental rapid-growth protein. Our character reluctantly puts on the kiddy cosmetics to please her parents and the next morning discovers she is a teen—transformations are grand, remember. That leaves us with a ten-year-old mind in an eighteen-year-old body. Our character, as you can imagine, discovers that being eighteen is not as much fun as she thought it would be. We will make it a comedy with a trace of drama (column #4). Our awkward eighteen-year-old is in the wrong place at the wrong time. Perhaps she goes to a nightclub and sees a crime she should not have, so bad guys need to rub her out. The storyline involves lots of chases. Maybe she gets saved by her ten-year-old male classmate who, the day before, she would not even speak to because she thought he was far too juvenile. We can call the story *Lip Gloss,* a girl's version of the movie *Big.* The matrix is nothing more than a kid's world, organized in a way to spur the creative mind onward. I will now dispense with the column numbers, but as we go through the examples, think about the character, the fantasy, the source of fulfillment, and the genre implied by each example.

Perhaps our hero is a twelve-year-old boy, a genius really, who is obsessed with creating a machine that will smash the barrier to heaven, thus to reunite him with his mother who recently passed away. But as fate would have it, he miscalculates and ends up in hell, and must use every ounce of nerve, agility, and smarts he has to get back again, while attempting to survive an array of hideous demons. Perhaps, in the end, his mother's heavenly spirit helps him escape. We can call it *Heaven Quest*.

Or perhaps our kid, a small, weak boy too often bullied by the whole world, stumbles across ancient tablets that are, in effect, a user's manual for the human body. Perhaps it was left there by an alien race that either created or pitied us. Imagine our hero's shock when he discovers that this user's manual instructs him on how he can achieve supernatural powers by focusing his body's electromagnetic fields. Let us make it a comedy. Crossing his fingers in a certain way while rubbing his head allows him to levitate things. Rotating his eyes while he belches allows him to knock things over. If we have him save the world (and his pride), that is a great fantasy for all kids. We can title it *User's Manual*.

Perhaps our hero is a lonely, tween-age girl named Faith who lives in a secluded countryside with her grandmother. Feeling very much alone in her locale, and excluded by the city-kids at her school, our rather smart tween uses her computer to map the entire DNA chain. She uses the knowledge to create strange and magnificent animals—her only friends—that she then uses to populate the forest near her home. She brings one of her strange beasts—a cross between a squirrel and an owl—to school to show others and, she hopes, gain popularity. While she gains a few momentary friends she also gains the unwanted attention of the school's unscrupulous science teacher, who desires her discovery for himself. At the story's climax, our heroine is chased across the countryside by those who wish to steal her secrets, and she dashes toward the only place where she knows her true friends, the animals she created, will protect her: her forest. We can call it *Faith's Forest*.

Notice that for each story idea, I included bits and pieces of a kid's world, culture and interests—from cosmetics to heaven to aliens to forest animals. Each "cue" already holds special meaning for the child, is emotionally laden from the start, and provides the story with context. In fact, more complicated matrices would include a listing of all those elements that a child connects with his life: such as school; leisure activities; parents and family; toys and games; music; friends; and themes such as pirates, space, dinosaurs, and so on. All of this provides more interest, added emotion, and more relevance.

For example, perhaps an imaginative girl who loves to draw is given a special chalk by a wizard that allows her to fall into any mural she creates. It sounds pretty good to live in a world of your own design, until she realizes that all worlds have dangers lurking to grab her, and she must use her wits to return to the real world. Perhaps in the end she learns that our world is not so bad after all. It sounds like an episode for Nickelodeon's program "Are You Afraid of the Dark?"

Or perhaps our underappreciated hero is a boy who constructs a threadlike material that will fly. Then he weaves it into a carpet in preparation for his school's science fair. Yes, it does become his magic carpet. Then we add an evil villain, perhaps even a foreign power, who desires his invention and puts the world at risk. We might have the beginnings of an afterschool special, a comic book, or an episode of the program "Family Matters." We can call it *Carpet Power.*

Other story-based matrices can also contain an array of pressure points, that is groups of people or professions that can be at odds with each other: teachers versus principals, students versus administrators, girls versus boys, parents versus children, older siblings versus younger siblings, popular kids versus unpopular kids, team A versus team B, kids versus villains, brothers versus sisters, rich versus poor, kids versus nature, and so on. The possibilities are endless.

In most good stories, a moral will also be communicated. At the end of the tale, our hero will understand the consequences and responsibilities that often come with a fantasy that is achieved; thus he is a bit wiser and mature at the end of the story than he was at the beginning.

In the end, the matrix does not create any ideas, you do. Its purpose is only to help tickle your creativity, and that of your colleagues, so that you have plenty of ideas to consider before deciding on which to pursue. As will be explained in chapter 18, research can help you select the most promising ideas.

Story-Based Ever-Cools

To help your story become an Ever-Cool, you must first make it a success in the medium of your choice (e.g., books, television, film). That is the most difficult part. To help make it extend to more stories, create an extendible element. That can be a hero who survives, an evil that is not completely destroyed, or an icon or device that connects the old to the new. As cited earlier, George Lucas created the *Star Wars* saga in *episodes* that painted a much larger story, strung over many films. Gene Roddenberry's "Star Trek" also created a connecting device. In the continuing "Star Trek" saga, captains and their crews can come and go, as can villains. Even some ships will come and go, as will some space stations. But Star Fleet is likely to remain, as will the tales of one particular ship named the *Enterprise,* commanded by a captain who boldly goes where no one has gone before.

Ideas That Transcend

It used to be that a great movie idea was a great movie idea, and a great toy idea was a great toy idea, and a great book idea was a great book idea, and that was that. They seldom overlapped. But the walls fell down between categories. Movies became toys, toys became movies, both turned into television programs, which became bed sheets, pencils, or whatever. Licensing, in fact, began to explode in the late 1970s and early 1980s with such characters as

Strawberry Shortcake, Care Bears, and so many others that eventually adorned pillow cases and curtains and became cereals and toys. Suddenly, everyone seemed to be leasing the rights to use legally protected names, graphics, logos, sayings, or likenesses.

I refer to ideas that can hop from category to category as Ideas That Transcend. Many of them began in comic books and film before making their way around to the other various mediums. Teenage Mutant Ninja Turtles, for example, was a comic book for five years before it became a cartoon, a line of toys, and eventually movies. Others were television shows, such as "The Flintstones," years before they became films. Other ideas that transcend are simple characters that are transported from one category to another. Such is the case when the Trix Rabbit, and the associated colorful aspects of the Trix brand, were carried from the cereal category into the yogurt category.

The most powerful ideas that transcend have some common elements. First, they powerfully fulfill a child's needs in the original category where they were born. They must win there, first. Once accomplished, such ideas can hop into other categories more easily if they are based upon a central story. That story reveals how a sympathetic character jumped over hurdles to achieve some burning need. Such a story and its characters elicit strong emotions that kids can identify with and hence want to express outwardly via objects like apparel and toys. Stories that transcend well are also those that not only target kids, but appeal to the kid in all of us. *Star Wars* did that. So did *E.T. The Extra-Terrestrial.* Such stories can be enjoyed at the movies by adults and kids alike, can be the focus of a play pattern for toys at home (often good versus evil), have a theme song or songs that are enjoyed in the car tapedeck, and have unique characters (good and evil) that kids identify with when they see their appearance on drinking glasses, T-shirts, lunch pails, or on the label of their next canned pasta.

Many ideas will not meet the above criteria and, therefore, will not be able to transcend. That is fine. We should
not stick space aliens into the film *Casablanca* just so we can
squeeze a toy line out of it. But if a storyline idea can be
easily constructed about your product idea, it could have
serious and profitable repercussions. It is worth the time to
consider this when developing product ideas even for the
most mundane categories.

But ideas that transcend are dangerous as well. If you
purchase a license, then you depend greatly upon somebody else's success before you can enjoy yours. Such is the
case when marketers line up to license the elements of a
film a year before the film is released. Things do not always
go as planned. Disney's *The Hunchback of Notre Dame* is such
a case. *Advertising Age* reported that "Disney's latest annual
'event' film has produced unspectacular box-office results
to date and, as ticket sales continue to decelerate, toy industry insiders claim retailers and department stores are can-
celing big orders for *'Hunchback'* merchandise."

Many times marketers, in actuality, fall victim not to failure, but to expectations. After all, *Hunchback* did a very
respectable $77 million at the box office after only 24 days.
But all eyes were on the previous successes of *Toy Story* and
The Lion King. The bane of expectations was echoed in a
comment made to *Advertising Age* by a spokesperson for
Burger King, "The distribution of [our] kids meal premiums for *Hunchback of Notre Dame* has fallen slightly below
our very ambitious expectations."

Managing expectations is a skill in itself. So when the
marketer picks a license, he must ensure that he is fully
aware of many variables, including the license's target audience, its image, other supporting partners and the dollars
committed, the history of the license, its potential longevity,
the timing of it, the competitive environment, as well as
how well the license fits with his brand's own identity and
objectives. He must stay connected to the pulse of the target

audience. He must stay connected to studios, early sales information, gossip, anything that might tell him whether he is about to buy a diamond or a lump of coal.

Final Thought

Everyone has ideas for kid-related products and stories, but few of them are worthy of pursuit. The ideas that are begin with a notion that touches a child's heart. And by beginning your search in a place deep within children's psyches, their world, and their culture, you can increase the odds of coming up with a winner. If matrixing helps in that process, use it.

Brand Challenges

- Have you established a "routine" idea development process, or is it ad hoc?

- Are you employing idea generation techniques that will help you create a consistent flow of ideas, ones that touch a child's heart?

- Are you on the lookout for ideas that transcend?

See, Daddy, see? That's the one I want!

17

Develop Kid-Appealing Advertising

*I do not regard advertising as entertainment or an art form,
but as a medium of information.*
—David Ogilvy
Ogilvy on Advertising

ADVERTISING has a special function in the marketing mix,
for its role is to bring the core essence of the brand to life,
thus illuminating the emotional need it satisfies, the role
the brand plays in a kid's life. And in so doing, it is the
end result of years of labor, attention, resources, and
worry that began with the conception of the brand itself.
So it is frightening to realize that after all that effort, your
brand's whole reason for being often gets reduced to just
thirty seconds' worth of a television commercial. That is a
lot of pressure for a scarce thirty seconds' worth of copy
and pictures.

ADVERTISING: *The action of attracting public attention to a
product or business*

The pressure, then, to ensure advertising's effectiveness
is immense, and you can feel that pressure at any advertising agency. Opinions fly; arguments erupt; debates over
strategy and creativity ensue; bursts of feverish activity are
commonplace. Still, kid-directed advertising is developed
by passionate people who care about kids, about putting a

smile on a child's face, about touching a child's heart. It is about creating happiness, eventually served up in a splendid piece of advertising that excites a child with a brand that fulfills some emotional need.

And kids, by and large, like the advertising they see. For them, it is a catalog of wishes, for advertising alerts children to the items that are available in the huge world beyond their doorstep. In so doing, it brings them exciting "news" of either totally new brands or re-inventions of established ones. The newness of such adds mightily to draw a child's interest. So unlike adults who might leave for the bathroom or the refrigerator the moment a station break comes, kids often wait around to see the commercials. They examine them. They are entertained by them. They discover what is new, what is cool. They learn the jingles, copy, and action. They use the advertising to decide which brands are worth the effort of a request. Then they yell across the house or drag a parent back from the refrigerator to the television and exclaim:

> "Mom, that's the Barbie doll I want."
> "You see—McDonald's now has *Dalmatians!*"
> "Dad, can we pleasssse go see *Hercules?*"
> "I want Waffle Crisp cereal, Mom. It's cool!"

Effective Advertising

On the surface, "effective" advertising seems to be a subjective evaluation. A piece of advertising can be strategically sound and creatively break through and sell a $100,000,000 of product, but if the goal was to sell $120,000,000, the advertising may well be judged a failure. Alternatively, another campaign can beat its sales goal by 20 percent, but if the powers that be hate the advertising on judgment, then it can also be deemed ineffective. The reasoning goes that if it was a better commercial, sales should have been over goal by 30 percent. The subjective nature of this evaluation is compounded by the fact that the success of the advertising is so closely linked with the innate appeal of the brand itself, it is often difficult to disentangle the appeal of each.

Despite such subjectivity, the following are some general guidelines for developing effective advertising based upon hundreds of cases over many decades and product categories. "Effective" for our purposes will be defined as advertising's ability to clearly bring the brand's reason for being to life, thus touching a child's heart and inspiring a child's request. And when such advertising evolves year after year to reflect kid culture, it can help the brand stay Ever-Cool.

Strategic Synergy

Effective advertising has a single-minded, strategic synergy; that is, the key elements embodied in the advertising work seamlessly together to communicate a focused and relevant, brand-differentiated message. This strategic synergy is depicted in the Synergy Model in Exhibit #17-1. The Synergy Model begins at the top and moves clockwise, beginning with communicating the brand's most relevant and unique product feature(s), which delivers the brand's emotional benefit, which is expressed in a meaningful brand name, which is brought to life in an advertising execution. When linkage between these components is strong, advertising is more likely to be effective. So naturally, when the linkage is weak, advertising is more likely to be ineffective.

Hence, advertising effectiveness is highly related to marketing decisions that began long before the first advertising concept was presented, such as the brand's innate appeal and the selection of an appropriate brand name. Advertising, after all, serves up the entire brand package.

Let us review the model in more detail. Advertising effectiveness begins with identifying the brand's single

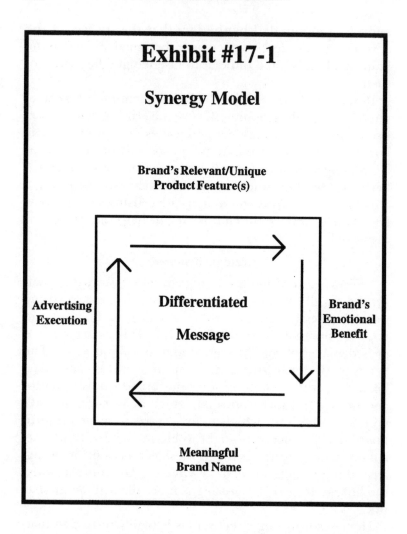

Exhibit #17-1

Synergy Model

Brand's Relevant/Unique Product Feature(s)

Advertising Execution

Differentiated

Message

Brand's Emotional Benefit

Meaningful Brand Name

most relevant and unique product feature(s), as expressed by the child. The feature(s) could be a taste, a texture, a sound, a fit, a play pattern, a style, a visual appeal, a heritage, a character, an attitude—all depending upon the nature of the category and the brand. Olympic Gymnast Barbie doll has agility, provided by a "tumbling ring" that allows her to do cartwheels and somersaults. Of course, she comes with a gymnast-themed outfit as well.

The key feature leads to an emotional benefit that touches the child's heart. Olympic Gymnast Barbie doll offers play patterns born of aspirations, achievement, and pride. Other brands tap into one or more of the many emotions detailed in Part II, such as the fun that can be derived from gaining control and independence, resolving fears, being silly or outrageous or gross, receiving and giving of love, achieving victory and mastery or a fantasy, and others. Each emotion, in essence, denotes the role that a specific brand plays in a kid's life. The product features are a mere means to that end. Says Noah Manduke, senior partner and group account director at Ogilvy & Mather Los Angeles, "The magic is in the product, but the fun is in the play."

It is this relevant product feature and emotional benefit delivered to a specific kid audience (i.e., parent-focused kids, gender-focused kids, transitional tweens) that constitutes the advertising's strategic underpinnings. If done well, the advertising is on the path to being cool.

Either the key product feature or its emotional benefit is then expressed in, and linked to, the brand name. Thus, the brand name helps communicate a meaningful message in and of itself. Olympic Gymnast Barbie doll denotes precisely what this Barbie is and does. Names can also benefit from being not so descriptive as they are attitudinally whimsical. The *Frisbee* brand name is one example.

Finally, the key feature(s), its emotional benefit and its brand name, are brought to life through the advertising execution. For Olympic Gymnast Barbie doll, the commercial featured only those items and activities central to being an Olympic gymnast, such as the Barbie doll's ability to spin and perform gymnast moves, her outfit, and importantly, an emotional payoff as she wins the gold medal! Other features of the doll were not included because they were not supportive to the single focused idea of the product itself.

Finally, computer-generated imaging brought the Barbie doll's persona to life.

In this seamless effort, a focused point of view emerges that communicates what the brand has to offer: key product feature(s), emotional benefit, reinforcement by a brand name—brought to life with the advertising. The more often these elements work together, the greater the likelihood that the child will be able to understand the brand's advantages.

If any of these elements is weak, as cited earlier, the whole message will be weakened. If the brand does not have a product feature(s) kids like over and above competitive offerings, the advertising will suffer. If there is no emotional benefit, the advertising will suffer. If the brand name has no linkage back to either a product feature or the emotional benefit, or if the name is hard to remember or too cumbersome to say, the advertising will suffer. If the advertising execution is unfocused, attempting to communicate too much, or using executional elements that interfere with rather than reinforce the main message, the advertising will be weaker. And in the mesh of confusion, kids will deem the advertising, and the brand it conveys, as uncool.

Advertising Execution

The advertising, as stated, brings the core essence of the brand to life. More often than not, it will do so in a thirty-second television commercial since that remains the primary means of reaching kids. There are many ways to *execute* the advertising. David Ogilvy, a legend in the business, would always search for what he called the "big idea," referring to an approach that would grab attention and communicate the brand's benefit in an intriguing, unique way. There are many places to look for that big idea in a kid's world, and below is a partial list. Each is possible of communicating the brand in a way that kids may deem cool.

Importantly, each of these approaches is not mutually exclusive, but can be used in combination.

Cool Demonstrations: This approach uses a dramatic demonstration of the brand's benefit. Recall the milk commercial cited in chapter 7, which in thirty seconds demonstrated its benefits by showing a girl grow into a young adult while drinking milk, all the time discussing the benefits that milk has to offer her growing body (i.e., the rational benefit) which, implicitly, will increase her confidence and help empower her (i.e., the emotional benefit).

Cool Problem/Solutions: This approach shows the problem and then reveals the solution provided by the brand. The Sega brand of videogames ran advertising that depicted a small boy being picked upon by a pair of bullies until he got Sega. Then, of course, he received respect.

Cool Characters: Real or imagined characters are also used to endorse brands: Ronald McDonald, Chuck E. Cheese, etc. Sugar Bear has been craving Post Golden Crisp cereal for so many decades that most kids know he "just can't get enough" of them. Such characters must serve to communicate the brand's benefits, or they end up overshadowing the brand.

Cool Testimonials: This approach uses loyal, real-life users to endorse the brand. Or, as executed in drug prevention campaigns, you can also show past users or nonusers *not* endorse drugs: "Just Say No!" The people used in these testimonials must be considered cool by kids.

Cool Spokespersons: Under certain situations, celebrities can be used to endorse the brand: Michael Jordan for Nike, Amy Van Dyken for Wheaties. These spokespeople are not just cool celebrities, but celebrities who have a natural association with the brand they endorse, linked by sports, ability, or attitude. Because celebrity endorsements for kids brands are frowned upon by industry watchdogs, celebrities are not used in advertising directed to kids ages twelve and younger in a way that would identify them through their professions with the product or service. However, kids younger than twelve often become familiar with which celebrities are associated with which brands via exposure to adult marketing efforts.

Cool Fantasy Worlds: Fantasy worlds or settings can bring a brand's benefit to life by showing the role a brand might play in the fantasy. McDonald's ran a campaign, referenced in chapter 7, that showed a kid obtaining his dream of joining the NBA, getting an agent, and after the game, going to McDonald's, of course.

Cool Cultural Worlds: In this approach, the advertising makes use of popular music, language, sports, and relevant mood, attitude, or action to associate the brand with a kid's life. But to do it well, *cool* must be born out of the brand, not just slapped onto it. When rap music first became cool, for example, it was used in many commercials for many brands whether it applied or not. It often got in the way of the brand's features and benefits, and plenty of kids in focus groups told us as much. The brand must be the focus of attention. A good example is the long-running advertising campaign for Post Fruity Pebbles cereal and Post Cocoa Pebbles cereal, to be described shortly.

Advertising Campaigns and Ever-Cool

All of the executional approaches outlined, and others, strive to blossom into campaigns. That is, a series of advertisements constructed with and related by common elements that can live beyond the current commercial. This allows kids to see, over time, a common point of view with regard to the brand. Common campaign elements can be a tagline, a song, a character, an attitude, or a recurring demonstration or situation, to name a few. Nike's tagline of "Just do it" reflects a timeless attitude, and a personal challenge, that has survived many years and across many pieces of advertising copy. It is made current with a string of celebrity athletes and updated executional style that helps keep the advertising and the brand Ever-Cool.

Interestingly, very few advertising campaigns are Ever-Cool in themselves. That is, few of them are constructed in a way that allows them to be easily refreshed to reflect shifts in trends and fads. More often than not, advertisers completely overhaul their advertising every few years because the campaigns relied too heavily on a certain fad that eventually waned. Rap music, as cited earlier, was one of these. When such fads become uncool, there remains no common advertising element that survives, and a new campaign exploration commences.

This makes advertising-related Ever-Cools all the more precious. The advertising campaign developed for Post Fruity Pebbles cereal and Post Cocoa Pebbles cereal is one such Ever-Cool. The campaign uses Fred and Barney, of Hanna-Barbera's "Flintstones," as two of the common campaign elements. The advertising highlights the brand's taste appeal by way of product emphasis as well as Barney's timeless struggle to trick Fred out of his cereal. Yet the campaign stays fresh year after year by drawing heavily from kid culture. When sky surfing became a popular sport, Barney jumped from a plane (a Pterodactyl, actually) and sky surfed toward Fred to snatch the cereal from him. When dinosaurs became once again popular with kids, Barney dressed up as a T-Rex to trick Fred out of his cereal.

This campaign, nurtured by Ogilvy & Mather since the 1970s, has been a huge success. It satisfies several timeless emotional needs driven by the brand's taste and shape appeal as well as the excitement derived from Fred and Barney's friendly competitiveness to obtain it, yet it was constructed in a way that makes it easily refreshed with contemporary themes. "A long-running campaign is like a marriage," believes Alice Germanetti, the creative director responsible for the advertising. "A certain amount of familiarity offers kids security and mastery. Too much and they start fooling around with someone else." For the Post Pebbles brand, the balance has been achieved, for few advertising campaigns in the world have lasted as long, making it one of the few advertising-related Ever-Cools.

Advertising Dilemmas

Advertising is never clear-cut. There are few absolutes, and so debate ensues. Here are some of the contested issues.

Brand Focus versus Cool Executional Elements: In an attempt to gain a child's attention, advertisers use a huge array of devices such as music, computer graphics, animation, fantasy settings, characters, and unusual camera angles and techniques. Arguments arise about whether the brand itself is being given enough attention, as opposed to the attention-getting techniques that are thought to be cool. In general, all techniques should be used to showcase the brand and to help bring to life its key feature, benefit, and the role it plays in a kid's life. If the techniques do not do this, they are wasted.

A good example of advertising techniques working in concert with product attributes was the introduction of new varieties within the Popsicle brand from Good Humor-Breyers Ice Cream. The new varieties included new swirled shapes, colors that changed when you licked them, multiple colors and flavors stacked on top of each other, and so on. "When the boy tasted Popsicle in the advertising," began Myron Lyskanycz, managing partner with Ogilvy & Mather Chicago, "he or his environment immediately transformed in a way that paralleled the product itself. With Popsicle Sherbet Cyclone pops one taste created an actual cyclone within his room. With Popsicle Lick-a-Color ice pops, as the product changed colors, so did everything else around him." The unique product and parallel advertising approach worked. Says Lyskanycz, "Each new Popsicle product featured in the campaign ended the year ranked as one of the top five U.S. novelty ice-cream introductions of the year in sales."

An important note is voiced by Dick Newman, vice-president of marketing at Good Humor-Breyers Ice Cream. "The sky's the limit for kids with colors, shapes, and concepts. But don't mess with taste. They know what they like and they won't compromise. Don't get so excited with the trappings that you forget that if it doesn't taste the way kids want, it won't go anywhere." Said another way, never forget your brand's reason for being, either in new product development or in advertising.

Simplicity versus Cool Complexity: Some executives say advertisements have to be as simple as possible so that the youngest child within the target age group can understand them. This requires simple language and more simple forms of humor. Others say this makes you lose the older children who will deem this approach as juvenile and then deem the brand too childish. Older kids want faster-paced, cooler, more complex images, they say, as well as more adultlike humor such as satire.

In many cases, you want all your communications to be simple to understand, but served up in an older, cooler attitude, thus to give the younger children something to aspire toward without alienating older kids. In some cases, you might be able to have appeals to both, such as the way Bugs Bunny's physical exploits will entice younger viewers while his wit will entice older ones. This is harder, but it is worth trying to achieve. Also keep in mind that kids absorb more than adults do. So test, as you might be surprise at how much the younger kids actually comprehend.

Words versus Cool Music and Song: Some executives prefer music and sung copy to create a cool attitude. Other says it is in the interest of clear communication to have all key copy spoken plainly rather than sung. The answer to this debate is—it depends. Music and singing can add much to attitude development, particularly if the song is so enticing that children begin to sing it over and over. Many of you can probably sing the words to the Oscar Mayer

Wiener Jingle. Still, if the lyrics are hard to understand, or if they are asked to bear the burden of communicating a complex piece of copy, then they are best spoken plainly. In fact, a combination of sung and spoken copy can be quite successful.

Boy versus Girl Casting: When children reach the gender-focused and young tween ages, (somewhere between five and ten years old), the separation of sexes is immense. So girls are placed in commercials for girl-related brands and boys are placed in commercials for boy-related brands. Brands that target both sexes during these ages are often more effective when they use boys in the spots and not girls. Boys are often turned off by the presence of girls, whereas girls are not turned off by the presence of boys. But this, too, is a generality. At times it may be worthwhile to use girls as foils, as someone who will react to a boy being gross, for example. Similarly, boys can be used effectively as foils for girls. When kids become older tweens we begin to see that boys' interest in girls increases, so that showing each may be fine, and cool, depending upon the specific circumstances.

Adult Cool versus Kid Cool: Adults often make the mistake of thinking they know what kid cool is. They do not. I do not, even after researching kids for nearly twenty years, because cool changes constantly. The best we can do is to satisfy a timeless emotion, dress it up in a way that fits current kid culture, and then test it with kids so that we are sure we did it right. If we overdo cool, they will catch us. I have heard over and over again from children that the kid actors in one commercial or another were stupid because they were "trying to act cool." It is a tough act, and it is the same with kid slang. You can do research to determine what slang kids are using today, and use it in your commercial only to discover that by the time your commercial runs the slang is no longer cool. Thus, it is best to *show* cool, not *say* cool. Then test to make sure you did it right.

Here are a few more thoughts, and a reminder or two, when developing kid-directed advertising.

- Make it amazing. Give it energy. Make it humorous, if appropriate. Make it something kids will talk about on the playground.

- Show the kids in the commercial having fun *in relation to* and *because of* the brand.

- Make the brand the focus of attention—the hero—by showing the role the brand plays in their lives.

- Never talk down to kids. They are typically smarter than you think they are.

- Include a "magic moment" if it applies. That is the surprise moment in a commercial when an exciting feature is suddenly revealed.

- Be honest, never promise anything that the brand cannot deliver.

Brand Challenges

- Is your advertising cool?

- Long before you even think about advertising, are you laying the right strategic foundation via the brand's product feature(s), emotional benefits, and brand name?

- Does your advertising have strategic synergy, that is, are all the elements working together to support the brand's key feature and emotional benefit?

- Is your advertising truly a campaign whose elements can be pooled out over time into refreshed, more contemporary executions? Is it Ever-Cool?

That will be all for today, kids. I'm sure the folks behind the mirror know your opinion of our new flavor.

18

Develop a Research Program

The only fence against the world is a thorough knowledge of it.
—John Locke (1632-1704)

MORE THAN 90 PERCENT OF KID BRANDS FAIL. Some fail because their core idea was not strong enough relative to competitive offerings. Said another way, they were not the most successful in touching the child's heart. Even if the core idea was brilliant, many eventually become extinct because the idea was not re-invented or updated in subsequent years to accommodate current trends and fads. Others fail because the advertising missed the mark or the retail trade was disinterested. Still others fail because of dumb luck and bad timing. As Cervantes wrote in his masterpiece *Don Quixote,* "Merit does much, but fortune more."

Market research simply increases the odds of success. It does not guarantee success, for nothing can in a business where attitudes can change monthly, if not daily. But research can prevent you from making some classic mistakes, such as thinking that you know what a kid really wants. You do not. Says Alan Fine, a specialist in family, entertainment, and youth marketing who spent some fifteen years with Mattel, "No matter how much you think you know about kids, you're not a kid . . . so expect the unexpected."

Decision Making

The objective of research is to help the marketer make better, more informed decisions that help launch new brands and contemporize existing ones. And since every marketing plan entails hundreds if not thousands of decisions, market research can be employed to aid judgment at many critical decision points to ensure that a kid's voice is heard, that the plans reflect what children think is cool.

Unfortunately, most companies use research in an ad hoc fashion. They do some pieces of research, but not others. Hence, there is no process to ensure that the most critical decisions have kid input before other decisions follow. This can be deadly. Exhibit #18-1 shows the key steps in the research process, each of which corresponds to key marketing decisions when launching and rejuvenating brands. The objective of this process is to provide the right kid-related information at the right time, thus to attain Ever-Cool.

Kid Scan

The first stage in developing a successful marketing program is to understand what is happening in a kid's world. This will provide tremendous input for subsequent ideas and decisions. At the onset, a "kid scan" should reveal how much influence your specific audience has in the decision-making process. As cited in chapter 1, this will help the marketer decide whether the audience is the child, the parents, or both.

Kid Environment

Providing that children are the prime audience, the marketer first needs to know more about their interests. This entails knowing what is cool and what is not, particularly in those high-interest categories such as films, music, celebrities, television shows, videos, fashions, sports, videogames, and toys. Secondary research sources can be purchased that

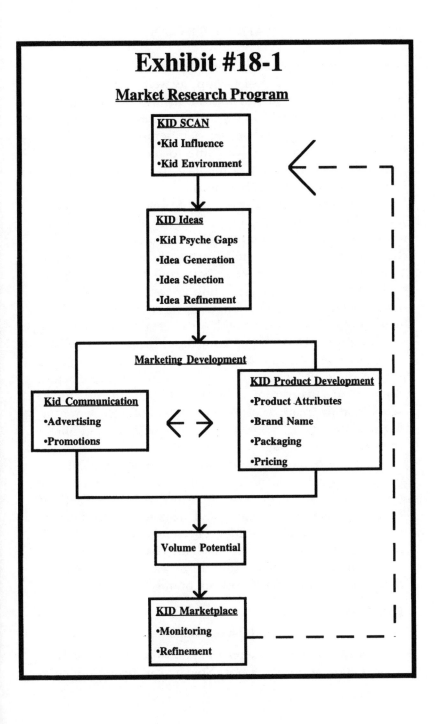

Exhibit #18-1

Market Research Program

KID SCAN
- Kid Influence
- Kid Environment

KID Ideas
- Kid Psyche Gaps
- Idea Generation
- Idea Selection
- Idea Refinement

Marketing Development

Kid Communication
- Advertising
- Promotions

KID Product Development
- Product Attributes
- Brand Name
- Packaging
- Pricing

Volume Potential

KID Marketplace
- Monitoring
- Refinement

will help the marketer discover what is cool. These include reports from The Zandl Group, as well as a plethora of trade magazines that provide the listings of the top box-office grosses, top-selling toys, top licenses, top videos, top performing artists, and more. Demographic and cultural trends can be had by subscribing to such publications as *American Demographics*. Kid media habits can be obtained through services such as Simmons.

It is also important to continually talk with kids face to face. There is no substitute for looking a kid right in the eyes and asking him what is hot and what is not, as well as how he feels about his neighborhood, his world, his life. And of course, how he feels about your brand. It helps to see not just what he says, but how he says it, the attitude in which he delivers it, the language he uses. To do so, it is often helpful to connect with kids a couple times a year, oftentimes quarterly. Some companies bring children into their place of business continuously. Others conduct group discussions with kids at an independent focus-group facility. Some hire cultural anthropologists to observe kids at schools, at the mall, or on the street. Still others are venturing into the on-line arena to ask kids questions and obtain their responses through cyber space.

This knowledge will help marketers generate ideas and make decisions regarding how to contemporize existing brands to attain Ever-Cool; for they will discover their brand's perceptual strengths and weaknesses, the licenses or tie-ins they should consider, the trends they should hitch their brand to, the nuances needed to freshen their advertising, and so forth. Such knowledge will also lay the foundation for creating new Ever-Cool brands.

Kid Ideas

Kid Psyche Gaps

At this stage, the marketer will know the trends, the fads, what is cool, and what is not. Now he can review the competitive environment and look for the psyche gaps—that part of a child's psyche not currently being satisfied by a competitor. If there are no gross foods, then that might be an opportunity for a food marketer to satisfy boys in that arena. If there are no videogames that target the girls' need for achievement and mastery, then there exists an opportunity for such an idea. If there are no apparel options that delight a child via touch, taste, sight, sound, or smell, then an opportunity just might exist for an apparel maker to satisfy a sense ignored by others. If there are no upcoming films that satisfy a child's fantasy of transforming into someone bigger, someone richer, someone stronger, or someone with ultimate control, then there might be an opportunity for such an idea.

Finding psyche gaps is one thing, developing a kid-appealing idea is another. So once the gap is identified, it is necessary to develop many potentially cool ideas in hopes that one will successfully fill the gap.

Idea Generation

This is where matrixing comes into play, as demonstrated in chapter 16. It will help the marketer mix and match all the elements of a kid's world in hopes of finding a way to fill the psyche gaps. A cereal developed specifically for an eight-year-old girl's desire for beauty, for example, might come in the shape of rings and necklaces that she can wear before, of course, she eats them. That is one among hundreds of possibilities. The matrix will also challenge its user to discover ways to make the new brand Ever-Cool.

Idea Selection and Refinement

Once the marketer has developed various ideas that target the kids' psyche gaps, then it is time to take the ideas to the specific audience to gain reactions. This will help the marketer narrow his options and fine tune those that show promise. Typically, product concepts can be expressed on one sheet of paper with a rough drawing, a tentative brand name that reflects the core feature or benefit, a short paragraph summarizing what the product is or does (its key feature and benefit), and any necessary information regarding flavors, shapes, and the like.

The Cool Chart: To begin, these concepts are brought to children in focus-group discussions whereby several groups of six children or so are exposed to the ideas. The children can be asked to place each idea on a "Cool Chart." The Cool Chart is a long, wall-size diagram that has a long line with an arrow at each end. One end reads "Very Cool" while the other end reads "Not at All Cool." The middle of the chart might read "Sort of Cool." The moderator asks kids to vote as to where along the continuum each idea falls. It is a very insightful exercise, especially when you add a successful, competitive brand already in the marketplace. That way you have a comparative "control" from which to better judge your ideas. The chart makes kids think and compare. It is especially insightful when a trained moderator inspires the children to debate about where each idea falls on the chart, which are cooler than others, and why. Personality profiles can be built to help the marketer understand the dimensions of the brand idea beyond the physical characteristics. Such probes provide a deeper understanding of the child's perception of the mystic cool, and how your new brand idea stacks up against it.

Says Bob Hay, management supervisor at Ogilvy & Mather New York, "The beauty of the Cool Chart is that it instantly prompts kids to express how they really feel about a brand or an idea. They become enthusiastic, involved, and downright passionate about where something should be placed on the chart and why it should go there."

Cool Chart research will help narrow the options from a few dozen down to a handful. This research will also help the marketer fine tune each idea based upon the children's reactions, likes, dislikes, and suggestions. Potential brand names and packaging concepts can be explored if available. It is also here that the marketer strives to understand what the single most important feature and emotional benefit truly are, thus to ensure the ideas are focused from the very beginning. This is the beginning of Ever-Cools.

Next, a more rigorous quantitative "concept test" would be warranted on those remaining concepts to help select the best possible idea. The concepts would be exposed to hundreds of children across the country to determine which has the greatest innate appeal relative to competitive offerings.

Marketing Development

Once the idea makes it this far (as few as one out of a hundred typically do) it is time to develop and finalize the many elements of the marketing mix from the brand's product features to the advertising.

Product Attributes

Brand prototypes are now developed, and the actual physical composition needs to be finalized. The nature of the fine tuning depends, of course, on the nature of the industry. For food products, taste tests will fine tune the final formula. Is it too sweet, too sour, too crunchy, too gooey? Toys might be put into play-testing scenarios to ensure the appropriate age grading, ensure product performance, and gain insights into play patterns.

The research to accomplish these objectives often begins with small-scale qualitative studies such as focus groups and ends with larger scale quantitative surveys, depending on needs and resources.

Brand Names

If not already finalized, the brand's name is set at this stage prior, of course, to packaging development. Often, children are exposed to alternative names and simply asked what each name connotes, the likes and dislikes of each, which best fits the new brand, and which is the coolest. The Cool Chart can be helpful here, as well, by letting kids rank the alternative names along the *cool* continuum.

Names that tend to do well are short and communicate something about either the brand's key product feature or its emotional benefit. Nickelodeon's Gak, that slimy substance that boys just love, is a great name. It is short and to the point, with a promise of yuck. Play-Doh is a good brand name as well. So is *Goosebumps,* and the name of the film *Toy Story.*

Packaging

Packaging alternatives can also be tested to see which best "pops" off the shelf, communicates a brand message, and conveys *cool.* In one study of board game packages, we simply allowed groups of consumers to view mock retail shelves containing a variety of games, inclusive of a new packaging concept. Then we asked questions about which box "popped out" and why. It is important to determine if the packaging communicates an aura consistent with the overall brand idea. Quantitative research techniques use large, matched samples. If there are two packaging alternatives under consideration, for example, each package will be placed in a separate but identical competitive array, which is then exposed to two different but matched sets of consumers to determine how many consumers pick each alternative package in a simulated purchasing environment.

Pricing

Kids think in terms of cool, not price. So pricing is typically a parent issue, one in which they play the important role of gatekeeper.

Prices are typically set with a manufacturer's profit margin in mind, while being alert to competitive offerings. Pricing is also a strategic weapon. In markets with low-priced commodities, there may exist room for a higher-priced item that delivers better quality, and vice versa. It becomes a game of price points, defined by levels of value. Varying prices points can be tested to determine the falloff of volume as the price is raised. Hence, demand curves can be built that will reflect, in large part, the parent's role as gatekeeper.

Advertising

Alternative advertising concepts can be developed for the new brand and existing brands and exposed to kids via focus groups or quantitative research to determine which best conveys the brand idea in a cool way, while stimulating purchase interest (a child's request).

In the focus-group phase, children can be exposed to the advertising concepts and asked to rank each on the Cool Chart. The advertising concepts may be in many forms depending upon the level of "finish" necessary for the advertising to convey its message. This level of finish can range from a concept board (a key, drawn visual with copy) to a full storyboard (multiple drawings with copy reflecting the action of the commercial) to an animatic (a videotaped storyboard) to a photomatic (a videotaped storyboard using photos instead of drawings) to rough-live advertising (a commercial using videotaped actors in a simple set).

The objective of this research is to help the marketer eventually select an effective piece of advertising that will break through clutter, communicate the name of the brand, its key feature and benefit, and do so in an cool way that will elicit a child's request. If the marketer can discover an advertising approach that can do all this, while being easily refreshed each year, even better. That is the path to Ever-Cool advertising.

Promotions

Marketers can also bring promotional ideas to children to determine which can help our new brand have a successful launch, while conveying *cool.* And when done year after year, the right promotions can help a brand stay contemporary. As a preliminary screening tool for promotion ideas, the Cool Chart can work here, too. Should we run a promotion next summer with Sea World or with Knott's Berry Farm? Should we put a sample of Nickelodeon's Gak in our cereal box or a toy figure from Disney's *101 Dalmatians?* Should we run a promotion in which a dime of every box sold goes to save the whales or to support local schools? The best promotions are those that not only convey cool but also enhance the values inherent in the brand.

Volume Potential

Once the key elements of the new brand's marketing plans are decided upon, a final volume potential test is conducted across hundreds of kids and their parents to determine financial viability. Some methodologies actually give children a fixed amount of money and ask them to "buy" the products they want from a mock retail environment that has competitive offerings. Products such as foods require estimates of both trial and repeat* to arrive at sales projections. In such cases, parents and children who state that they would probably buy a product are often asked to take it home, to try it, and then to provide the researcher with information regarding how much they would buy in a typical month. The trial and repeat measures are then used to estimate sales. The above analysis will also help marketers determine if their new entry will expand their total sales or merely cannibalize sales at the expense of current lines. This is very important when the new product is not a new brand per se, but a new item within an existing brand. In the end, the marketer ends up with quantifiable, projectable estimates regarding the innate appeal of the brand

*When new products are being developed, trial estimates refer to the percentage of people who might initially buy the product. Repeat estimates refer to how much of the product they will buy thereafter.

relative to current competitive offerings. This research can also reveal further suggestions for improving the brand before a test market, if warranted.

Although this can all be rather technical from the researcher's standpoint, what the child is actually requesting, buying, and using in this research—which results in volume estimates—is a brand that touches his heart. It is nice to keep that in mind.

Kid Marketplace

After all the above key decisions, and many more lesser ones, are made, the brand is launched into the world with all the fanfare of a child's birth. Advertising communicates the brand's reason for being, with a name that, by itself, is enlightening and fun. Related promotions add excitement and coolness. Packaging pops off the shelf and communicates the benefits inherent in the brand. The product attributes of the brand then deliver what is promised.

Now we wait, hold our breath, and see if we succeed, for there are plenty of other marketers who believe their current offerings are every bit as enticing as ours. Also, there were many brands that were suddenly launched when ours was, which adds to the intrigue. Monitoring this marketplace becomes a critical means of determining if we are succeeding and why or why not.

Sales: Our company's own sales figures will tell us if we sold adequate volume to the trade. Several syndicated research sources track retail sales through to the consumer. This will tell us if we are winning in the marketplace, and if so, from which competitors we are drawing sales. But it will not tell us why sales are rising or falling.

Diagnostic tracking: Syndicated research such as consumer panels can be purchased to track not just sales, but repeat rates, household composition, and some purchase dynamics (e.g., who bought, who used) thus adding to our understanding of a brand's impact. Elaborate telephone tracking studies can also be employed to do a more exhaustive job in obtaining information on awareness of your brand and the perceptions of it (e.g., coolness) relative to competitive offerings. Media analysis will provide insights into the media elements that worked and those that failed.

All of this data is invaluable because it will direct the marketer to the area of the marketing plan, year in and year out, that might warrant attention and refinement. Such monitoring, along with the on-going "kid scan," becomes an ever-present part of marketing's continuous effort to make better decisions and to attain Ever-Cool for various brands.

Tips on Kid Research

I have always found kids easier to research than adults. Adults do not easily give you straightforward, honest answers. Instead, they try hard to be politically correct by giving the researcher socially acceptable answers. They might also try to "please" the interviewer, which results in them overrating a brand. Other times they might overexaggerate the negatives of a brand because it is their opportunity to put an advertiser on the hot seat. Yes, researchers have ways to pierce the walls of adult rationality, but it is tricky.

While children, too, can be difficult to research in ways cited above, they tend to be more straightforward and honest. If a boy dislikes a product idea you put before him, chances are he will tell you it is "stupid." If he really hates it, he will tell you it "sucks." And that is that, no politeness, nothing held back. He is not worried what you will think of him or how his comments might hurt your feelings. Girls will be just as straightforward, although perhaps not as graphic.

If, on the other hand, kids like something they see, you will know it immediately by the eagerness of their posture, their attention, and the gleam that dances in their eyes.

Then they will say it is fun or *cool.* Those two words are for-ever current, although other faddish slang might be used as well, such as *hot, rad, sweet,* or something else by the time this book is published. Hence, kids are a researcher's dream. Says Tom Meredith, director of research for The Disney Channel, "Kids are very intelligent and mature, but on a smaller scale. In many ways, I think we can learn more from them than they can from us." Conducting research among them, however, does present a few difficulties.

Self-expression: When researching kids on the younger end of the spectrum, say ages five and younger, trouble can ensue due to a child's inability to express himself, limited by either shyness or vocabulary. This is often resolved by screening for the child's ability to carry on a conversation with an interviewer. If they are neither articulate or forth-coming, they are not selected. When conducting focus groups, children can also be recruited with a friend so that they come to the research with a person they know, which takes some of the fear out of the interviewing session. Once the study begins, easy warm-up questions are asked to put the child at ease. These might ask children to describe their favorite food or to describe what their family did on their last vacation. If the research is in a focus-group setting, kids might also sit on the floor with the moderator.

Reference group pressure: The older the child is, the more intense this pressure becomes. In research conducted with groups of twelve-year-old girls, for example, it is not unusual for a girl, when asked a question of the moderator, to glance at the other girls in the group before she answers. In effect, she is desperately trying to read their expressions before she commits to calling a brand or idea cool or not. So, when speaking to groups of children at a time, it is best to have the older children write responses before they dis-cuss them out loud. It can also be beneficial to conduct the research with only one child at a time, thus to eliminate the pressure entirely. On a related point, it is always best to separate boys and girls. If they are together, boys will show off, and girls will clam up. Children in focus groups should also be grouped by similar grades. That way the children are on equal footing for the most part.

Boredom: A younger child's attention can wane quickly. When it does, the information you may try to collect beyond that point is often wasted. To resolve this, researchers create activities that will keep a child's attention high. The Cool Chart is one such technique.

Another method is the fantasy toolbox. It includes tools such as storytelling, drawing pictures, and pretending. So, it not only helps prevent boredom, but it aids self-expression. If your brand is Baskin-Robbins, for example, and you want children to discuss purchase dynamics and perceptions of your brand, you might begin by asking children to tell you a story about the last time they visited your store; who in the family asked to go to Baskin-Robbins and why (versus competitive offerings); how they got there; what they did once inside; what they ordered and why. Ask the child to give the story a beginning, a middle, and an ending, as all stories have. Ask him to draw pictures representing the visit and of those things he liked most and least. Ask the child to pretend that Baskin-Robbins came to life for just one day as a real person and to imagine what Baskin-Robbins would be like: age, sex, cool or not, fun or not, popular or not. This can be very insightful for determining brand attributes and imagery relative to competitors. You will begin to see the role your brand plays in a child's life.

Abstractness: Children cannot respond in the abstract. They need to see; to touch; to feel; to hear the product, advertising, or promotion that is under research. The more concrete the marketer can make the stimulus, the better. So real prototype products, detailed drawings of such, or videotaped advertising concepts can make a difference in a child's understanding of the idea, which provides more accurate findings.

RESEARCH: *Neither panacea nor poison*

All of the issues cited above, and their resolutions, depend on the objectives of the research and the tradeoff of time, cost, and quality. There is no absolute right way, only methods deemed more appropriate given various circumstances. The goal, always, is to help the marketer make decisions resulting in the creation of lasting kid brands. The emphasis here is on the word *help*. Research cannot replace analysis, sound judgment, and gut intuition—it can only provide information to add to the marketer's arsenal before he makes decisions.

Some marketers worship at the feet of the research idol and seldom take a step unless their decisions can be research "justified"—in other words: paralysis. Others detest research and prefer to always follow their gut. After recommending research be conducted among children to guide an important advertising decision, Freddy Bee, senior partner and director of client services at Ogilvy & Mather Los Angeles, was told by one resistant client, "I don't want *children* telling me what my advertising ought to be!"

I have found the middle ground to be the most fruitful. I know of several kid brands in which research declared them to be failures, yet they went on to be huge successes. I have also witnessed marketers ignore the research warnings and introduce products to certain death. Good research is typically predictive about 70 to 80 percent of the time, if you are lucky. The rest is left to chance, to gut instinct, and to fortitude.

Brand Challenges

• Is your brand supported by a research program that delivers the right information at the right time to help you successfully launch new brands and then to make them Ever-Cool?

Nah, I didn't murder anyone. I'm the guy who marketed those x-ray glasses you find in the back of comic books.

19

Attain Standards and Ethics

Children are our most valuable natural resource.
—Herbert Hoover (1874-1964)

CHILDREN HAVE A GREATER CAPACITY THAN ADULTS DO TO TRUST, to misunderstand, and to use products in ways not intended. They are also not as wise as adults as to the ways of commerce and the marketplace. Because of this, they are a special audience, indeed. In a marketer's rush to satisfy a child's needs and attain Ever-Cool, then, care must be taken to ensure that the child is safeguarded.

Of course, people disagree about the extent and definition of this "safeguarding." So this chapter will review a variety of opinions and issues facing marketing to children. They range from the most basic of topics, such as whether it is appropriate to market to children at all; to matters of quality, safety, and responsible advertising; to issues of degree and nuance, such as when does a story or play pattern become *too* violent.

Marketing to Kids

Some would prefer that marketers never design products for children, never talk to kids via advertising, and never entice a child with a special offer or promotion. Marketing is seen by them as plain and simple exploitation of our youth. This is the most extreme view, and it does not fully appreciate marketing's benefits.

233

The simple role of marketing is to create and develop brands that fill needs. In a child's case, these needs include comfort, safety, and fun in all of its dimensions. And most parents can attest to the hours of smiles that a simple yo-yo can bring to the child's face, the feeling of accomplishment that can come from a work of art molded from Play-Doh modeling compound, or the tender feelings of comfort that arise as a girl holds her Cabbage Patch Kids doll within her embrace on a dark, cold night. In the end, marketers sell smiles—not dolls, not trains, not videogames, not breakfast cereal—but smiles. Such toys not only provide fun for the child, but also provide greater convenience for the parent who may not have the time or the skill to construct a yo-yo by hand, make that modeling clay, or stitch that doll by himself. Most would agree, then, that the existence of such products is beneficial.

As it relates to the appropriateness of advertising brands directly to children, mothers in recent focus groups offered us a range of opinions. Some thought not, for they felt advertising sets unrealistic temptations and fosters materialism among children who are too easily influenced. However, most of the mothers in this, albeit, unscientific sample believed advertising directed to kids was acceptable because it provided information about what was available. And providing that it did so accurately, advertising was even viewed as a learning experience. "It's all part of teaching our children about life," said Melody, a mother of a three-year-old girl, "and about reality, limits, and boundaries."

But there is a price to pay for this lesson. For parents, this one included, can get tired of dealing with our children's requests. That is understandable. Yet a child's request is the result of a marketer doing a good job of offering brands that satisfy a child's emotional needs. In fact, for each request, there are nine other brands that fail because a child did not request them. More often than not, the winning manufacturer took the time and spent the resources to understand a child's desires.

This is not to say that all marketing directed to children is good. It is not. In the race to fulfill a child's needs things can go wrong. Products may not be safe. Advertising may be misleading. Promotions may use unreasonable pressure. All of which means that while marketing to children, in general, can be beneficial to kids and parents alike, we still need to be watchdogs in the specifics. We must ensure that the benefits of a brand far outweigh the potential negatives of its marketing program.

Product Quality

Many consumers complain about the lack of product quality. Product quality does matter, so much so that marketers seldom profit from making a product of poor quality. A poor-tasting cereal or cookie will suffer from a low repeat rate, and the brand will fail. If it is too sweet, parental veto will kill it. If it is a defective toy, it will be returned after Christmas. That not only casts a shadow over the manufacturer in parents' eyes, it also casts a shadow over the manufacturer in the retailers' eyes. This is not a good thing. So too will movies die after the first weekend if they do not touch the heart of the child in a fulfilling way. In fact, a study by *Teenage Research Unlimited* showed that quality was the number-one attribute that makes a brand cool in a teen's eyes. Teens must have learned that from somewhere, both from parents and from experience.

Many manufacturers include safeguards to ensure quality products. Toy manufacturers will conduct tests to ensure that a child can play or activate a toy in a manner desired without breakage. Food manufacturers test taste appeal. Movies are tested before opening weekend to get a read of appeal as well as to gain insights that help with finishing touches. Through all of this, manufacturers weigh not just quality, but value for the price paid, for consumers are often not willing or able to pay a higher price commensurate with the highest quality product. So the best quality, at the most affordable price, is often the goal. It is a balancing act.

And even with safeguards, products of poor quality get to the market, at prices that are too high. New toys will break. New food products will taste lousy. Movies will stink. When this happens, the public votes with their dollars by deciding which brands they will buy and which they will not. In a capitalistic system, this is one of the best messages any consumer can send to a manufacturer.

Product Safety

Products must be safe for the child to own and to use. This is not negotiable. The Consumer Product Safety Commission, in fact, works to ensure products are safe for children. In the toy arena, they send field inspectors to monitor the marketplace and search for toys that might create electrical, thermal, mechanical, chemical, or flammable hazards. Specific toy-safety standards, so reports the Toy Manufacturers of America (TMA), include requirements and test criteria for such items as: paint and other similar surface-coating material, pacifiers and rattles, toy-cap noise levels, electrical-thermal toys, chemistry sets, sharp edges and points, and small parts which could be swallowed or inhaled.

Such federal regulations, as well as toy industry voluntary requirements, are substantial. A plastic toy truck intended for a three-year-old, says TMA, may be subject to as many as fifty different tests. To keep in lockstep, manufacturers test products to ensure that such safety standards are met.

But when capitalism conflicts with safety, juries vote to compensate those harmed and punish those who are culpable. This makes all marketers think very hard about ensuring the highest safety possible.

Advertising

The Children's Advertising Review Unit (CARU), which is part of the Council of Better Business Bureaus, was established in 1974 by the advertising industry in order to promote responsible children's advertising directed toward kids. Its function is to review and evaluate child-directed advertising in all media. If it finds advertising to be misleading, inaccurate, or inconsistent with its guidelines, it seeks changes through the voluntary cooperation of the advertiser. The CARU guidelines provide many specific parameters that advertising should follow, which are related to such elements as copy, sound, visual presentations, product demonstrations, and violence. The intent is to ensure that the brand is portrayed accurately, that the benefits communicated are not overpromised, and that children are not harmed.

The guidelines go on to outline practices related to the use of extreme sales pressure, disclosures and disclaimers, comparative claims, celebrity endorsements, premiums, promotions, sweepstakes, and more. In addition, the television networks have lists of guidelines that they impose on advertisers. If an advertiser raises enough eyebrows, the Federal Trade Commission will get involved and prevent the advertiser from using certain techniques entirely, or the advertiser will run the risk of substantial fines.

Verification

These are all good practices and contain good advice. Hardly a soul would disagree with any of it. But it is in the details where controversy exists. Does a fantasy setting *truly* mislead children into thinking they can fly if they eat a certain cereal or do they realize that is just pretend? Do children *really* think that after viewing a certain milk commercial that they will grow muscles in thirty seconds after one glass, or do they realize that is just a demonstration of what *might* happen over many *years*?

Kids are often more savvy than we think. They are exposed to a wide range of fantasy stories and special effects that makes them alert to modes of communication. Also, parents make children wiser to the world by teaching them every cliché imaginable, not to believe everything they hear, not to judge every book by its cover, and so on. This heightens a child's alertness. Other interested parties get involved as well. Some years ago HBO ran a special program entitled "Buy Me That," presented by Consumer Reports. Directed to children, the program motivated kids to be cautious of advertising claims. In effect, its intent was to make children better, smarter, skeptical consumers.

Still, when a given piece of advertising is of concern, it is possible to test, to show the specific commercial in its entirety to kids, and then ask them questions about it. Done properly, the advertiser will determine whether its advertising is misleading, to what extent, and why.

Such research deals with perceptual issues. If, on the other hand, a concrete claim is being made in the advertising that arises from the manufacturing process, then consumer testing may not be needed or appropriate. One example might be the number of chocolate chips that a commercial promises to be in each cookie (say, thirty-five chips). If the manufacturer can prove at the factory site that thirty-five chocolate chips are placed into each cookie, then consumer research is not needed. Internal claim-substantiation, however, would probably be required.

Darwin's Law

In my experience, marketers rarely profit from a product of poor quality, one with a low value, one that is unsafe, or one whose advertising is misleading. Such brands are often out-competed in the marketplace, and the marketer ends up losing millions of dollars. If the brand does not fall to competition, it may well be attacked by consumer groups, politicians, legislators, or the courts. One toy manufacturer recently agreed to pay $280,000 to settle Federal Trade Commission charges that it violated an agreement not to run deceptive advertising. The strongest jury exists, however, in the court of commerce, where consumers vote with their dollars—which is why the great majority of brands fail.

Social Dilemmas

If resolving ethical issues were only as easy as counting the number of chocolate chips in every cookie, the debate could stop now; but, it is not so easy. Marketing's relationship with children has many gray areas, fueled by inconsistent, often conflicting opinions. Here are snapshots of a few of the most prominent battlefields and the opinions that abound.

Violence

Most people are concerned about children's exposure to violence in society, made even greater, many say, by marketers. Some say toy guns, for example, should not be sold for they believe that they preach violence, to which children should not be exposed. Many also assert that as programming has become more violent, children exposed to such programming have become more aggressive as well. One study conducted as early as 1956 alleged that four-year-old children who watched "Woody Woodpecker" cartoons were more likely to display aggressive behavior. Hence, many legislators and consumer groups desire to reduce a child's exposure to violence by restricting "violent" shows to times when most children would not be watching. These times are called *safe harbors*.

Others agree that violence is, indeed, a problem, but feel that significant issues arise when those in power attempt to decide the definition of violence. Is *Star Wars* violence or entertainment? What about "The Road Runner" cartoon? What about *The Wizard of Oz*? Hence, they argue that keeping violence away from children is best achieved via parental restrictions, self-regulating industries and rating systems, governmental "urging," and the marketplace, which will aid the development of products like the "V-Chip" to help parents regulate their child's viewing activities. Some even discount the research that supposedly demonstrates that violent programming makes children more aggressive. They cite flawed research methodologies and claim that even if there is a correlation between violent programming and a child's aggressiveness, it is very small compared to other contributors such as drugs, poverty, and the disintegration of the family. It seems our social researchers cannot agree.

Exposure to Adult Products

When a marketer's campaign for a potentially harmful product targeted to adults reaches kids as well, concerned voices are understandably raised. Some studies claim to demonstrate that cigarette smoking among youth is rising as the amount of money spent on cigarette advertising rises. For these reasons, Bill Clinton and the FDA have sought to restrict tobacco marketing in ways that avoids the eyes and ears of children. Others argue that such restrictions would result in a loss of adult freedoms afforded by the First Amendment to the Constitution. This is an important debate, one that will be fought by legislators, the courts, special interest groups, and parents. There are no easy solutions where freedoms are concerned.

Commercialization

Many parents delight when a live or cartoon program establishes a character that a child grows to love, especially those characters that the child can learn from and adore. But if a toy is introduced based upon the likeness of that character, some critics will argue that the program is suddenly not a program at all, but a thirty-minute advertisement for the toy itself. The opposite is also true: if a child expresses an interest in a Teddy bear, and then a program is produced based upon a Teddy bear, some will shout "exploitation!" even though a child could be delighted with both. In effect, the critics object to what I called ideas that transcend in chapter 16. Although both the program and the toy can bring hours of fun for the child, critics will charge commercialism. To address this, CARU and network guidelines will not permit a commercial for such a toy to be in or adjacent to the program in which its character appears.

School Infiltration

Debate also exists over where marketers market to children. "As tax caps and dwindling state and federal funds leave school districts financially strapped," reported *Youth Markets ALERT,* "corporations increasingly are filling the budget gap." But that has created concerns among some who assert that schools are allowing marketers to infiltrate the classroom. One report cited 110 instances of corporate-sponsored items such as posters, teaching aids, and books that are in the hands of 43 million kindergarten through twelfth-grade-age schoolchildren. Much of this material, although educational in purpose, bears corporate logos.

Many educators appreciate the corporate-sponsored teaching materials. Others, however, argue that our children should not be marketed to under the "guise" of education. They do not mind corporations bringing cash to those schools in need, they just wish the companies would go home before anybody recognizes them.

Targeting a Child's Heart

Some may be concerned that I have penned a book to help marketers better fulfill the needs that exist within a child's heart. I have even suggested that it can be beneficial to not just make a child more beautiful, stronger, or more in control in *actuality,* but it can also be of benefit to make them just *feel* that way.

Some might say that the world is a cold, dark place, and that a child who is small and weak should not be led to *feel* stronger if he is not, nor should a girl be led to *feel* prettier if she is not, for it might create unobtainable expectations. Yet as a researcher, I have watched from behind one-way mirrors as six-year-old girls have tried on children's cosmetics. And while some may debate whether the cosmetics made those precious little girls more beautiful in *actuality*, the girls all *felt* more beautiful, and told us so in words, in smiles, in the gleam of their eyes. I have witnessed small boys pretend to be superheroes, and in that moment they *felt* stronger and more powerful and ready to resolve evils against society. These children were not more powerful in reality, but they were where it perhaps mattered most—in their minds' eye.

Is this setting unrealistic expectations or is it igniting aspirations? Or perhaps, it is just a simple, harmless, fragile fantasy that brings a smile to young lips and makes the child feel good on the inside.

A Nation of Opinions

Our nation has an abundance of opinions on how to market to and protect children, stemming from all the issues cited above, and others. In part, the many opinions exist because each of us has a different and often changing perception regarding what is good and what is not, what is appropriate and what is not. And we are full of inconsistencies.

Because of our inconsistencies, we inadvertently send conflicting signals to our kids. We teach our children to honor Memorial Day for those who fought and died for our country. We teach them to honor bravery and the courage to stand up to aggressors. We tell our children a wide range of tales from David and Goliath, to Hercules and the Hydra, to those involving cops and robbers. But when these children act out what they hear and learn, playing good vanquishing evil in some version, it makes us uncomfortable.

Clearly, there is an invisible line that some marketers cross, and it is only apparent once it is crossed. For years parents tolerated toys, for example, with names like Slime, Gak, and S.N.O.T., but when another manufacturer introduced products with names like Eye Pus and Projectile Vomit, they were pulled from the market due to protests from a suburban Cincinnati teachers' group. Even though most mothers will allow their daughters to play with Barbie dolls, some would rather Barbie be not so beautiful or glamorous. Yet when a less beautiful and less glamorous doll was introduced, few kids asked for it and few parents bought it. It failed. Others will fault the Mighty Morphin Power Rangers for using force to save the earth, yet you hear few complain when Superman does the same.

We cannot agree. This is why many believe that while marketers, the government, consumer advocates, and special interest groups all play important roles—the greatest role of all is played by the individual parent or caregiver who has the ultimate responsibility for a child's upbringing. The individual has the ability to veto those brands deemed harmful, to limit the amount of time children watch television or play videogames and as such, guide children in a manner that is reflective of parental beliefs and moral judgments. This is echoed in a comment from Lori, a mother of four girls, when asked if advertising directed to her children should be permissible. She said, "Yes, I feel it's fine. It is my decision to limit TV watching anyway. If I felt there was too much advertising I would limit TV even more."

Lori, along with millions of other parents, does not always have a popular job. But she is very much aware of the crucial role she plays in the overall marketplace.

At any point in time, then, given the push and pull of the various parties who strive to both fulfill a child's desires and to protect him in the process, we can probably say this: that the majority of Americans have, in their voice or their silence, voted, and that our nation has achieved the balance we desired in terms of allowing marketers to fulfill a child's many needs, while keeping the potentially negative aspects of marketing to a tolerable minimum.

Brand Challenges

- Is your brand setting an example in the industry for quality, for value, for safety, for advertising, and for ethics?
- Have you found that invisible line where meeting a child's desires comes at too great a moral price?

20

Create a Lifelong Relationship

World-Class Kid Brands

PAUSE FOR A MOMENT and make a mental list of the kid brands that are formidable successes, not a flash in the pan or a fad but brands with both longevity and immense proportion. There are only a few: Disney, Barbie, McDonald's, and Sesame Street. More recently we have seen MTV and Nickelodeon. There are perhaps a dozen or so more.

World-class brands have a couple of things in common. First, they have crafted a relationship with children based upon emotional benefits, not merely upon product attributes. Those in charge realize that their brands are not just physical substances made of film or plastic or potatoes or whatever. Their brands are more defined by aspirations obtained, fantasies fulfilled, or senses gratified. Such brands make a child *feel* something on the inside.

Such brands also touch a child's heart in multiple ways. A trip to Disneyland will bring the joy of fantasies fulfilled, the pride of adventures accomplished, and the warmth of friendly characters met. A trip to see a Disney film will intrigue and delight children with villains they will loathe and a sympathetic hero they will love. Nickelodeon's programming will allow a child to feel gross one moment and silly the next. Then Nickelodeon will make the child feel empowered by asking him to send in his vote for president of the United States. McDonald's will provide a tasty meal,

Mom!
Now can I play with my Barbie doll?

will pack it in a box full of contemporary premiums, and will then weave itself into the neighborhood with charities and community involvement that can mean much to those affected. These are the reasons why these brands were among the few that were referenced in multiple chapters, because each built many relationships with the child and touched many aspects of the child's heart in both timeless and contemporary ways.

World-class kid brands are also quality brands, for study after study proves that quality wins out. Hence, tremendous resources are expended to ensure that quality, however defined in a specific category, is reached and consistently maintained. Not only can parents tell the difference, but kids can, too. It matters.

Brand Stewards

World-class brands are also guided by someone, or a team of someones, who truly understand them. These are the men and women who, in Ogilvy & Mather terminology, are called "brand stewards." They are people who know the role that their brand plays in a kid's life. They know the emotional needs that their brands can satisfy, and they focus all their attention, their single-minded vision, toward ensuring that their brand lives up to its reason for being. They can see a promotion and declare in a heartbeat, "My brand wouldn't do that!" Or alternatively, "Yes, that's Barbie!"

Brand stewards are also ruthless. They protect their brands with the tenacity of bulldogs. This extends to the marketing plans they approve, the licensing deals they make, and the infringements they prosecute. They have an innate sense of total responsibility for the health and well-being of their brand, and as such, they will not give an inch. In spirit, they do not even work for the company that employs them so much as they work for the brand they helped to create and to develop. Some of these brand stewards work at a toymaker's bench. Some know how to add the ingredient of fun, in all of its guises, to a kid's food. Some make movies, write books, or develop programming. Others produce advertising. A handful become CEOs.

Brands, A Lifelong Relationship

Brand stewards also know the power of developing a brand relationship early on in a child's life. "Many marketers take for granted the importance of building brand relationships early," says Rick Roth, executive group director of worldwide client service at Ogilvy & Mather New York. "Yet when you build a strong brand relationship with a child, you will have begun a relationship of a lifetime."

That is right. Even though the day may come when children outgrow the functional benefits of your brand, the feelings they have toward it will remain, buried deep within their adult psyches. Then, years later when these adults have children of their own, they will come back. They will remember the relationship. And so concludes Rick Roth, "They will want their children to experience it too!"

At that moment, you will have achieved what most marketers seek in vain, an Ever-Cool of immense proportion. One of such longevity that it has become a link between generations, gladly passed down through the years from parent to child. That is when you will know for sure that you have been victorious in your battle to win a kid's heart.

APPENDIX
Recent Changes

The publishing process is one that requires a high degree of planning, preparation, and time. Rough outlines and sample chapters are submitted by hopeful writers. Such outlines are reviewed by equally hopeful, yet weary editors who are near-blind from scanning mile-high piles of competing outlines. If an outline is fortunate enough to be accepted by a publisher, it may take months before the outline becomes an acceptable manuscript. In crafting his masterpiece, an author will suffer many late nights at a keyboard, his tired eyes squinting at the blue haze of a computer screen, his stiffening fingers pounding out words that form sentences, paragraphs, pages, and chapters. Just when the case of pain relievers is nearly all gone, the manuscript is completed and sent off to the publishing house. They, in turn (the author hopes), will accept it, edit it, and typeset it over a period of months. After the typeset pages arrive from the typesetter, the proofs are read a final time for typos. Finally, the final proofs are sent to the printer, who will print and bind the book and add a cover. The publisher then sends the author's new book out into the real world, which is filled with people who will react with either applause, disdain, or worse—utter disinterest.

This is all to say that by the time the book makes its debut, the world has moved on a bit from where it was when the outline and manuscript were accepted. Many

months, sometimes years, may have passed. This is prob-
lematic for a book that discusses trends and fads, since in
the time it takes to get a book to market new fads appear
and old ones die. Some linger in between the extremes.
These last few pages were written after the manuscript for
Creating Ever-Cool was long put to bed. Here is a very brief,
mid-year 1997 look at a few prominent items that have
sparkled with the principles of Ever-Cool.

The film sequel *The Lost World: Jurassic Park* kept the
Jurassic Park franchise Ever-Cool by introducing us to yet
another island of terrifying beasts. The film made history by
breaking nearly every possible opening weekend record. It
grossed nearly $93 million in just four days. Why? Because
Steven Spielberg is a master filmmaker who is skilled at testing our nerves and tickling our fears. He knows where our
inner emotions live, and he touched them again with the
use of a timeless, enticing theme—rampaging dinosaurs—
made current by storyteller Michael Crichton, best-selling
author. My eleven-year-old son and I saw the film together,
and it touched that child in both of us who wants to overcome fears, to triumph, to be heroic. Interestingly, I did not
take my six-year-old daughter to see the film because I felt it
would be too intense for her. And yet, I couldn't help notic-
ing that other parents brought children who were even
younger than she. I thought back to chapter 19 and my
comments regarding the importance of each parent being
allowed to decide what's best for his children. To each his
own. It's a much better system than having governmental
regulators censor the creators and marketers themselves,
which would take many potentially splendid works of art
and entertainment from all of us.

George Lucas reintroduced a new generation of younger
moviegoers to *Star Wars* on the big screen in 1997.
Multitudes flocked to theaters to see the original trilogy,
episodes IV, V, and VI. It was a huge success because young
and old were able to imagine that they, too, were empow-

ered to control the "Force" and battle evil for control of an entire galaxy. It is pure emotional fulfillment. But the reintroduction of the *Star Wars* trilogy was only part of Lucas's plan, I'm sure. Certainly, the seed is being planted for when the new films, episodes I, II, and III, come to theaters. Lucas is once again applying the Ever-Cool formula to ensure that two generations of moviegoers have tasted the sweet nectar of *Star Wars*, which bodes well for the future of the franchise. When the first of the new films finally hits the box office, the sheer magnitude is apt to blow the doors off of theaters worldwide. My family will probably be the first in line; may the "Force" be with us.

Some recent reports show that sales of older *Goosebumps* titles are slowing down a bit. Executives at Scholastic Corporation must be scratching their heads and trying to think of ways to keep the Goosebumps brand at its amazingly high sales level. Among other things, they are trying to extend the brand's excitement via promotions with other brands such as Pepsi-Cola, Taco Bell, and Hershey. I bet that even if sales trail off a bit, which is fairly typical after the initial, dizzying hype fades, *Goosebumps* is going to be with us for a long time, scaring young readers for many generations of kids. It has all the earmarks of an Ever-Cool and will be so if properly managed.

Beanie Babies, a bean-filled stuffed baby animal brand from Ty Toys, became a huge success. It touches a part of us that wants to nurture, wants to love. Recognizing the potential to tie into the craze and to remain Ever-Cool in the process, McDonald's put Beanie Babies in its Happy Meal. They sold one hundred million of the bean-bag animals in less than two weeks, according to one source. McDonald's, in effect, tapped into the toy's popular nurturing appeal in order to keep the McDonald's brand looking current.

Nurturing also went high-tech when virtual reality pets came to America. Tamagotchi is a small computerized, egg-shaped game from the Bandai Company. An owner of a

Tamagotchi gives witness to the hatching of an egg on a small LCD screen. The hatchling becomes a virtual creature who must be fed, cleaned, played with, kept healthy, etc. The better parent you are, the longer Tamagotchi grows and remains happy and healthy. Interestingly, early reports indicate that boys as well as girls own them (a lot of adults, too), suggesting that the game appeals to a boy's nurturing side in a way that boys would accept, via computerized game play. My own two kids are caring for the same Tamagotchi. Their patience at playing parent is already wearing thin, so they asked me to adopt their baby. I told them that I already had two Tamagotchis by the names of Matt and Megan, and I wasn't about to care for another.

Are these new pets fads or Ever-Cools? Will they simply be used by other mega-brands such as McDonald's to make themselves look cool, or will they be able to develop a long-term brand franchise on their own? Time will tell, but I expect it to be a difficult task to freshen up these nurturing toys in a way that will make them seem new again. We will see.

Mattel introduced "Share a Smile Becky" doll, a friend of Barbie. She is a fashion doll who uses a wheelchair. It is a nice demonstration that a disability can be portrayed in a positive light. The toy manufacturer showed sensitivity to the many circumstances that children find themselves in and then reflected this specific circumstance in a way that was beneficial. Such efforts foster goodwill for Mattel, as well as Ever-Cool for the Barbie brand.

Parker Brothers is gaining early success with its special entry of The Monopoly Game: Star Wars Edition. Instead of buying hotels and houses to get rich, players buy X-wing fighters and other ships instead, a related form of wealth and power for those who love *Star Wars*. Parker Brothers is demonstrating that even a brand as tried and true as MONOPOLY can benefit, and help itself remain Ever-Cool, by tying into current kid culture, trends, and fads.

In *Creating Ever-Cool*, I applauded Nintendo's ability to

allow a child to control his own world. I also predicted that Nintendo 64 would fly off the shelf. A combination of the advanced nature of the system and the shortage of Nintendo 64 machines at the end of 1996 increased its "coolness" via exclusivity. The latest reports suggest that Nintendo 64 did in fact fly off the shelf. The June 9, 1997, issue of *Business Week* reported that Nintendo is once again at the top of its game. Nintendo had sold some 2.6 million "N64" machines in North America, taking 50 percent of the market. As early as April 1997, seven of the top ten videogames in the U.S. were for N64. This is amazing given that there were very few games available for the advanced machine. Nintendo's next task for maintaining Ever-Cool: Get more, quality games for N64—fast!

The rest of the year will unfold with movies, toys, foods, and many other products directed toward kids—all competing to empower them, nurture them, gratify their senses, help them gain control, resolve or tickle their fears, allow them to reach a fantasy, touch a dream, or wish upon a star. To find a list of those brands fortunate enough to emerge on top, you need search no further than your local newspaper and assorted magazines. The winners are always prominently displayed. Or better yet, just ask your kids or those on your street. They will know.

"That's right . . . but how does he know that?!"

What Karen, a seven-year-old, asked a friend when she overheard Gene Del Vecchio talk about the timeless truths that live in a child's heart.